BLOODY VALENTINE

Douglas Skelton is the author of six previous books, including *Deadlier than the Male: Scotland's Most Wicked Women, Blood on the Thistle: A Casebook of 20th Century Scottish Murder* – which was later adapted for the stage by Glasgow's Citizens' Theatre – and (with Lisa Brownlie) *Frightener: The Glasgow Ice Cream Wars*. He has written extensively on crime for Scottish newspapers and has appeared in a number of television documentaries.

By the same author:

*Blood on the Thistle: A Casebook of
Twentieth-Century Scottish Murder*

*Frightener: The Glasgow Ice Cream
Wars* (with Lisa Brownlie)

*No Final Solution: Unsolved Scottish
Crimes of the Twentieth Century*

A Time to Kill

*Devil's Gallop: Trips into Scotland's
Dark and Bloody Past*

*Deadlier than the Male: Scotland's
Most Wicked Women*

BLOODY VALENTINE

SCOTLAND'S CRIMES OF PASSION

DOUGLAS SKELTON

BLACK & WHITE PUBLISHING

First published 2004
by Black & White Publishing Ltd
99 Giles Street, Edinburgh

ISBN 1 84502 004 9

Copyright © Douglas Skelton 2004

A CIP catalogue record for this book
is available from The British Library.

Printed and bound by Creative Print and Design

CONTENTS

ACKNOWLEDGEMENTS

There are always people you should thank – and always people you forget. So thanks to the following and apologies to those I've omitted. I didn't do it on purpose. Or maybe I did.

Thanks to the staff of Edinburgh Central Library, Glasgow's Mitchell Library, Inverness Library and the National Archive of Scotland for their assistance.

To Mark Sweeney and Alan Muir of the *Scottish Sun* for all the help and information.

To Sean Milne at the *Scottish Daily Mirror* for the same.

To Gary McLaughlin for his help with the illustrations.

To Eddie Murphy and Elizabeth McLaughlan because, if I don't, there'll be trouble.

To Karin Stewart and Katie Bell for always being the first to buy these things.

To my wife Margaret for the endless cups of tea.

To the staff at Black and White who put up with my moaning and often haphazard ways.

To the staff of the *Cumnock Chronicle* and others at the *Ayrshire Weekly Press* – and one in Paisley – too numerous to mention by name, who put up with a lot. You know who you are.

DS

INTRODUCTION

They're tricky things, emotions – can't live with them and there's no chance of any sort of life without them. It's all a question of control. Some find keeping their emotions in check difficult while others find it all too easy. Some believe it would be better if there were no emotions at all but what a cold and soulless world it would be if that were the case. Others keep too tight a rein on their feelings, pushing them down in the belief that nothing can get through. Because, if nothing gets through, then nothing can touch you and, if nothing can touch you, nothing can hurt you.

But they are still there – those feelings – building up, growing in power. And then, dangerously, they can burst out. All those pent-up emotions and frustrations – all the rage and fear and hurt and pain. In most folk, they escape as anger or black moods but, in some, they manifest themselves more physically. These people hurt themselves or others. They cause pain mentally – and physically. For those people, emotions are demons that whisper to them in the night, taunting them, urging them to do harm.

Love, it is said, conquers all but the demons are more than a match for it. They have names too: Hate, Envy, Suspicion and Jealousy. These are the emotions that can twist a once-loving relationship into something dark and dangerous, something lethal. There are others that come not with a sly snarl but with a sigh. These are the demons that force us to turn against ourselves and they, too, have names: Shame is one, Regret is another. Like their whispering cousins, they are insidious, sneaking into the mind like a cancer, eating away at all reason and logic until there is nothing left but dark thoughts and darker deeds.

In this book you will find stories of people who were visited by

7

these demons and gave in to their murderous murmurs. The French have a term for such deeds – crime passionnel – and, in France, it is a recognised defence in cases where one spouse murders another after discovering infidelity. There is infidelity in these pages but I have taken a broader view of the term. Most of the crimes included here have one thing in common, though – most are murders committed by people who once meant something to each other until the demons came a-calling. There is passion here, certainly, but also calculation and cruelty. Breaking up may have been hard to do but murder was often easy. There are men who turned against wives or lovers or killed their rivals in love. And there are women who killed their men or were somehow involved in such desperate acts. One thing is certain – when it comes to murder, gender is no barrier. Not all men are thoughtless and callous, despite what some women may think, and women have not cornered the market on compassionate and caring natures – again, despite what some may think. The Y chromosome is not a prerequisite for cold hearts and bloody minds.

A couple of the cases here are not quite so clear cut. In one, a woman was found strangled but the man ultimately convicted of the crime may not have laid his hands on her. In another, a learned man schemed to dispose of his wife but circumstances got in his way and the plan failed. In a couple of others, it could be argued that the victim got what he deserved.

Emotions can propel good people to do evil things. Good people can cause pain, anguish and grief. The whispering demons can take an ordinary person and force them to commit extraordinary acts. Jealousy can turn into rage and rage into frenzy and soon someone is lying dead. But these people are not evil. Evil, if it exists, lies in the careful planning of a death. The devil, as they say, is in the detail.

So turn the page and meet the demons . . .

BLOODY VALENTINE

1

CLERICAL TERROR

John Kello

'Thou shalt not kill.'

According to the King James version of the Bible, it's up there at number six in the top ten of commandments. For centuries, it was number five but the Protestants relegated it when they split one commandment, the admonition about having no other gods and worshipping graven images, into two. It's a perfectly straightforward commandment. You don't kill – period. But there is another version. It states that 'Thou shalt not murder' and is there to excuse the pious for those unfortunate periods in history when they have been forced to slaughter all and sundry because they worshipped God in a different way or simply because they were a different colour and happened to be in their way. But the favourite version tells us simply that it is wrong to kill. There is no qualification to the effect that 'Thou shalt not kill unless thy victim is of a different political persuasion/nationality/colour/religion to thyself'. There are, of course, scriptural justifications for killing that allowed religious leaders to exhort their armies to smite enemies hip and thigh. This led to all sorts of atrocities – not to mention genocide. At the battle of Doon Hill, the pious Oliver Cromwell, when faced with an attack by an equally pious Scottish force, told his men, 'Trust in God, lads, but keep your powder dry.' There were ministers of religion on both sides, some perhaps even in the thick of the fighting, for whom 'Thou shalt not kill' meant very little that day.

There are many tales of warrior monks, priests and preachers who have struck hard for their God in battle. Thankfully, though, there are few tales of holy men who have turned to murder for their own ends.

However, John Kello, who preached in an East Lothian village, was one who did.

By the year 1570, the turbulent sea that was Scottish history had pitched and tossed its people back and forth in a storm of religious strife. The beautiful Mary, Queen of Scots had lost her struggle with the Scots lords. She was Roman Catholic and they were, in the main, resolutely Protestant. Murder and vengeance had marred her reign. Romance and rape had scandalised it. And rebellion and, ultimately, defeat had ended it. On 13 May 1568 her cause was well and truly lost when her forces were quashed at Langside and, two days later, she stepped aboard a fishing boat to cross the Solway Firth heading for what she prayed was sanctuary in England. But if the Lords hoped her flight would end the threat of a resurgence of the Roman faith then they were wrong.

Her half-brother, James Stewart, Earl of Moray, became Regent of Scotland but he, too, had his enemies. In January 1570 he was gunned down in a Linlithgow street by James Hamilton of Bothwellhaugh, a supporter of the Queen, by then under the dubious protection of Elizabeth of England. The assassin's shot had been fired from the home of the Roman Catholic Archbishop John Hamilton who was later hanged without trial by Moray's faction. The power of Regent then passed to Mary's father-in-law, the Earl of Lennox, but the decision split the country and once again rumblings of armed rebellion could be heard in the mountains, glens and farmlands of Scotland.

But, while all these political wranglings were going on, life continued much as normal in the nation's towns and villages.

And so did death.

The village of Spott lies near the East Lothian coast, about four kilometres south of Dunbar. Even today it is small, with only around 200 inhabitants, but it and the area surrounding it has often surfaced in the historical ocean. Two battles were fought nearby. In 1296, Scotland's King, John Balliol, was showing a bit of backbone – stiffened, it has to be said, by his nobles – and defying Edward of England's demands for fealty. At Spott Burn, the Scots came off the worse in a bloody encounter with the English forces. And, in battle previously mentioned, in 1650, the Scottish force loyal to King Charles II was cut to pieces by Oliver Cromwell's Roundheads at the foot of nearby Doon Hill. Cromwell, it is believed, celebrated his victory in a mansion house in Spott itself.

Almost a century before, local laird George Home was accused of being part of the conspiracy to murder Lord Henry Darnley, Mary's husband. He was cleared of the charge and later, in one of the many lunacies of Scottish justice, he was back in court to help decide the fate of Archibald Douglas who was now charged with the same crime. In 1543, a city burgess murdered local priest Robert Galbraith in Edinburgh. His successor was none other than John Hamilton, who later succeeded Cardinal Beaton following his death in St Andrews at the hands of the Protestant Lords. It was John Hamilton who found himself at the wrong end of a rope in Stirling for his part in the assassination of the Good Regent Moray.

One John Kello followed him as shepherd of the Spott flock, this time using the Presbyterian cause as a crook. The reverend gentleman had no doubt been sponsored by the same George Home who had seen Scottish justice from both sides of the courtroom in the Darnley affair. Without knowing it, Kello's decidedly unchristian behaviour would later be used as a club to batter the Protestant cause.

Kello was an educated man of ordinary background. Born in Linlithgow, he was married to Margaret Thomson, a woman of common if not barren stock, for they had three children, son Bartilmo and daughters Barbara and Bessic. He performed his religious offices diligently and was a well-liked, respected, passionate and eloquent preacher.

However, he was ambitious. His post brought him little financial reward and his wife, although she was a loving and loyal woman, did not have the background or disposition that would aid him in his yearnings to rise to the top. His stipend of £100 Scots per annum was not enough for him so he speculated in some Linlithgow property and received a dividend. As he later wrote, 'This manner of dealing kindled in me a desire of avarice, which the Apostle Paul, not without cause, termed "the root of all evil".' Spurred on by the success of his initial venture, he bought some more land, this time nearer to home, but it failed to turn a profit and he found himself in debt. This, coupled with a disagreement with the Kirk over his income, created a certain degree of stress. He began to wonder if things might be easier for him if he were single. Without his wife he might subsist more readily on his meagre income. Without his wife he might even marry someone who could help further his career. Margaret was fine as wives go but, as wives go, he wished she would.

And then his eye fell on the daughter of a local laird. If he could marry into that family then his future was assured.

Demons, it seems, were murmuring in his ear. You can do better, they hissed. You can go further, they whispered. You can be more, they hinted – but not with Margaret on the scene. If you want the riches of the world, you have to be rid of her.

And so the reverend genteleman began to tell people that his wife was not of sound mind. He began to spread rumours that 'she was tempted terribly in the night' to do herself a mischief. But, in reality, the only mischief being contemplated was in John Kello's own fevered brain and murderous heart. Poison was his first choice but his wife proved too hardy a woman and the doses he tipped into her stew failed to have the desired effect. He was, however, not a cold-blooded murderer for, even as he began to prepare the way to her dusty death, he worked himself into such a state of anxiety that he fell sick. He confided the details of a dream that had plagued him to Dunbar minister Andrew Simpson. In the dream, he said, he was carried by a grim man before the face of a terrible judge and, to escape, he threw himself into a raging river. He was followed by 'angels and messengers' with double-edged swords. They struck at him with the swords but he ducked and dived out of the way until he escaped. That dream and his unwise urge to relate it to Mr Simpson would return to haunt him.

However, his ambition proved stronger than his conscience and he still resolved to rid himself of his cumbersome spouse. With his wife remaining hale and hearty despite the administration of substances, it was clear the subtle approach was not going to work – a more direct means would have to found.

On 24 September 1570, he saw his chance. It was a Sunday and, as she prayed in her bedroom, he throttled her with a towel. According to his own confession, even as he was squeezing the last breath from her body, she bore him no ill-will. She was glad, he claimed, 'to depart if her death could do me an advantage or pleasure.' This sounds highly unlikely and smacks more of a man trying to reassure himself, if no-one else, that his victim loved him so much she went willingly to her doom.

Having finally done for his loving wife, it was time to make it look as if her fragile mind had finally forced her to take her own life – just as he had been hinting would happen for almost two months. He hooked a rope to the ceiling, tied it round her throat and hoisted her up. Then he locked the front door from the inside, leaving the key in the lock, and left the house through the seldom-used back door of his study.

Next, he went to his church and preached to his congregation. Whether his blood was up after the brutal murder of his wife cannot be said. What can be said was that he was more passionate than usual in preaching against sin. After the service, he invited some prominent members of his congregation back to the manse. He may have used his wife's fictional state of mind as an excuse for the visit, telling the would-be visitors that their presence would raise her depressed spirits. Only he knew that it would take a miracle of biblical proportions to raise her spirit. Naturally, when the small party reached the front door, they found it locked so he led them to the back door. Inside, they found his wife's body dangling from the ceiling of her bedroom.

'My wife, my wife!' He cried. 'My beloved wife is gone!'

Affecting the demeanour of a grieving husband, Kello went into mourning. However, although his demons had led him to commit cruel murder, he himself was not so callous. His despicable act weighed heavily on his mind and he was not helped by a visit from Andrew Simpson, the Dunbar minister. Simpson told Kello he had analysed the dream and had come to the conclusion that he had murdered his wife. The terrible judge of the dream was God, the messengers chasing him represented Scottish justice and the water his own hypocrisy. Only by confessing would he save himself from the deep waters into which he had fallen. Of course, Andrew Simpson couched his analysis in spiritual terms but it is still an impressive piece of work – if it ever happened. What is more likely is that he had heard some rumour and witnessed Kello's conscience niggling at him. The ability to spot troubled minds at work through dreams would later form the mainstay of psychoanalysis but, in this case, it is likely that this was tacked on later to support the strength of the still-struggling Protestant religion.

John Kello considered his next move. After his conversation with his colleague from Dunbar, he knew there was some suspicion over the death. Now he had to decide whether to go on the run or stay and tough it out. Finally, he convinced himself that God was speaking through Andrew Simpson and set off for Edinburgh to confess his crime.

The wheels of justice may grind slowly nowadays but, in those days, they spun so fast they were in danger of coming off. His confession was heard and accepted. On 4 October 1570, without any further ado, he was sentenced to be hanged until dead and thereafter his body was to be cast into a fire and burned to ashes. The authorities were determined not hang around and the execution took place that very same day.

From the scaffold, John Kello preached his final sermon. He claimed he was sorry for what he had done but he hoped that the enemies of his faith would not use his transgression to excuse the failings of the Queen. (It was commonly believed that Mary had conspired to have her husband Lord Darnley murdered in reprisal for the murder of her secretary David Rizzio and also to leave the way open for her to marry her alleged lover, Lord Bothwell.) Although the demons of ambition and avarice had led him to his present situation, he denied any suggestion that witchcraft was involved. At the time, citing possession by some demonic presence was a common defence in such matters. The grim-faced men of God saw Satanic worship at every turn but John Kello was determined to scotch those rumours.

Finally, he exhorted the multitude who had turned up to see him die to 'measure not the truth of God's word altogether by the lives of such as are appointed pastors over you, for they bear the self same flesh of corruption that you do, and the more godly the charge is where unto they are called, the readier the enemy to draw them back from God's obedience.'

Soon after his death, 'The Confessione of Mr Johnne Kello, minister of Spott; together with his earnest repentance maid upon the scaffold befoir his suffering, the fourt day of October 1570' was published in Edinburgh. Kello had murdered so that he could perhaps better his position in life but he had inadvertently given the enemies of the Kirk a weapon to use against it. The idea behind publication was that the murderous minister's abject penitence would serve the religion well and hopefully confound 'the poisonous sect of the Antichrist' who had been writing about the case in other countries.

Of course, the Protestant Kirk thrived in Scotland. It was already too powerful for one killer cleric to damage. As for the commandment against killing, be it number five or six in the Godly pecking order, it would be broken many more times in the future by the Godly, if not by the ministers themselves.

2

THE WANDERER

John Adam

A pale moon blinked from behind skittering clouds as the tall man walked alone along the Highland track. It was a chilly night in late March and a snell wind whispered in the grass and sighed softly through the bracken. There were other rustlings in the undergrowth as nocturnal creatures rooted about after food and scurried away from potential predators. Further away, a sharp cry rang out as one of them didn't scurry fast enough and fell prey to a sharp-eyed owl. There was death out there on that lonely trail and the man reeked of it. He walked at a brisk pace, not just to keep warm, but also to put as much distance as possible between himself and the ruined cottage high on the ridge behind.

He had left the corpse of his wife there. He had killed her and left her there, her body hidden by a pile of stones. Now he had to get away from that haunted place and return to Dingwall, to his own fireplace, his own bed – and the other woman he called his wife.

The sight of a figure ahead startled him. He had not expected to meet anyone – not on such an isolated road and not at that time of night. His thoughts jumped immediately to the dead body he had left behind. He had not planned for the corpse to be recovered any time soon but, if it was and he was reported as being seen in the vicinity, then his own life would be forfeit. He climbed over a wall to hide and waited to hear the person pass by – but no footsteps reached him.

He peered over the wall but saw no one on the road. Perhaps he had been mistaken and the fleeting moonbeams had played tricks with his eyes. He set out again. Suddenly the figure reappeared and his flesh chilled and his hair bristled. He could not decide if it was male or female but he knew one thing – it was not of this earth. It was just a little way up the road, still the same distance from him as it had been at its first appearance. It stood there, a silent spectre briefly illuminated in the blinks of moonlight. Watching him. Waiting for him.

The man turned and ran away as fast as he could but, every time he turned, the figure was there, neither closer nor further away, always watching. By the time he reached the edge of Maryburgh, the man was exhausted, more through nerves than exertion, so he sat down by the side of the road and filled his pipe. By the time he had fired up the tobacco and exhaled the smoke, the figure was gone. Whatever it was – a manifestation of his guilty conscience, or some supernatural visitor – he saw no more of it.

He did, however, see his dead wife again.

Early in the morning of 10 April 1835, fourteen-year-old Jane Stewart and eleven-year-old John Campbell were the first to catch a glimpse of the dead woman. They and Jane's aunts, Margaret and Betty (aged twenty-eight and forty respectively), were on a new plantation on the heights of Kilcoy, a lonely moor on the Black Isle – which, confusingly, is neither black nor an island. They were replacing fir saplings damaged by recent frosts. It was hard, cold work so, after some time, the two youngsters decided to take a break in the ruins of an old cottage. Inside they found a brown glove lying on a heap of earth and stones. They thought at first it had been left there by a planter but then they discovered a piece of black gauze, like a veil, sticking through the earth. With the curiosity of children everywhere, they tugged at the piece of cloth until it would give no more. Whatever the material was attached to was buried under the rocks and earth. They called Jane's aunts over and one of them began to dig away at the ground with her shovel. The first thing they found was a shoe. Then they realised with a lurch that there was still a foot inside it.

The youngsters were sent to the home of William Forbes, thought of, locally, as a decent man, about a quarter of a mile away. They ran all the way and were weeping from fear as they reached his cottage at around nine in the morning. When the children arrived and told him their garbled story, the sixty-year-old was sitting cosily by the fire and he really had no great desire to step out into the cold spring morning. At any rate, from what he could gather all they had found was some old clothes. But Jane and John, gibbering excitedly in Gaelic, insisted that he come with them and see what they had found. So he reluctantly left his fireside and followed them to Kilcoy and up to the ruined cottage on the hill known as Millbuie.

When he arrived, Mr Forbes took the spade and gingerly began to dig deeper but, when he uncovered a leg, he decided not to proceed any further. He took young John and walked to the house of innkeeper Alexander Macdonald. 'There's a melancholy thing down yonder,' he told the forty-year-old publican. 'It's a dead corpse.' After trudging up to the tumbledown cottage, he and Macdonald carefully pulled away a large rock and uncovered the dead woman's head. They saw that her face was badly swollen and smeared with blood, which had streamed from her ears and solidified on the flesh. They realised they should not disturb the scene any further and so they covered the body up again as best they could, 'lest the dogs get at it'. This was a job for the authorities and the party of women and men headed to Dingwall, six miles away, to raise the alarm.

News of a dead woman on the lonely moor spread quickly and, naturally, excited the interest of a great many people. Soon not only the local procurator fiscal and doctor were up on the hill but also a vast array of what would, today, be called rubberneckers. These included the local schoolmaster, an army officer of the Middlesex Regiment, residing in the area on half pay at the time, and a local carter – cart and all. As the crowd watched, the doctors had the body completely uncovered and removed it to Dingwall Town Hall for further examination. The ground underneath, they noted when the body was taken away, was saturated with the woman's blood. Her face was swollen and of a livid appearance, her tongue was thrust about an inch from the mouth and blood had discharged from her nose and ears. They found discoloration under the right ear and that both lower jawbones were fractured near the mouth. Two lacerated wounds on the scalp corresponded to the shape of a stone found under the head but it was obvious to the medical experts that the woman had been beaten to death. They wrote:

> On dissection, the brain was distended with dark-coloured blood, but in no way sufficient to explain the cause of death. The brain was firm and natural in every part. The lungs were natural, the heart loaded with fat but not diseased, stomach contained a fluid like barley broth and contents of abdomen generally healthy. From our examination and dissection of the body we have no hesitation in stating it to be our opinion that death was caused by the violence of the blows the deceased sustained about the head.

So this was no accident – no wall had tumbled down on a poor traveller. The woman had been murdered. There were questions to be answered. Who was she? And what was she doing up on that lonely road in the first place? If they could answer those questions, perhaps they could catch her killer.

The handbill was printed in Dingwall on 11 April 1835 and distributed there and in nearby Inverness. It read:

> MURDER!
> Whereas the body of a FEMALE was found about 8 o'clock in the morning yesterday – FRIDAY – the 10th instant, in the ruins of a hut within the new Plantation on the heights of Kilcoy, bearing such marks of violence as leave no doubt she was cruelly murdered.

21

APPEARANCE OF THE BODY

The BODY is apparently that of a married woman about 40 years of age; 5 feet 7 inches high, stout in figure; dark brown hair, mixed with some grey hairs, long at the back of the head, cut short over the forehead; wore a false front or curls of dark brown hair; coarse, flat features, thick lips, small nose marked by small pox; had a scar from the centre of the forehead downwards across the nose, and left cheek, 4 and a half inches in length, apparently occasioned by small pox, or a burn.

DRESS

The DRESS was a black silk velvet bonnet, lined with black silk Persian, trimmed with black silk ribbons; a net cap, a black figured bobbin net veil; a mantle of claret coloured cloth, bound with black satin; a check verona handkerchief; a small crimson merino shawl with light border; a purple or puce worsted gown (lindsey woolsey or winchey of home manufacture) trimmed with velvet; a puce figured silk band; a light blue petticoat, and an under dark blue petticoat, both home made woollen stuff, a pair of coarse blue worsted stockings, white in the toes; cloth selvage garters; shoes such as usually sold in shops, mended under the toes and heels; a cotton shift, marked on the breast with the letters JB; a coarse flannel jacket; a pair of drab jean stays; a pocket made of printed cotton, tied with a piece of blue striped tape, and containing four-pence of copper, and a small pill box marked 'J. Mackenzie, Chemist and Druggist, Forres'. The last word scored through, wore a plain marriage ring marled 'Gold' on the inside, on the 3rd finger of the left hand; and gloves of green kid.

PLACE WHERE FOUND

The PLACE where the body was found, is at the top of the Millbuie on the heights of Kilcoy, in the Parish of Killiernan or Redcastle, County of Ross, and between 200 and 300 yards in a straight line eastwards from the house of Alexander Macdonald, Changekeeper, which stands close to the Parliamentary Road leading over the Millbuie.

The Public are earnestly requested to communicate to the Procurator Fiscal of Ross, Dingwall, any circumstances which may lead to the discovery of the name and usual residence of the deceased, and of the person or persons by whom she has been murdered.

The body lies in the Town Hall of Dingwall, and it will be kept uninterred until Wednesday the 15th instant: to afford an opportunity of identifying it.

In a house in Dingwall, a quarryman, known to his neighbours and workmates as John Anderson, returned home that night to find his young English wife Dorothy filled with the news of the gruesome discovery. The rumour was that the dead woman was the wife of a shepherd, for there was a wedding ring on her finger and why else would she be in such a desolate spot? 'How I feel for her husband, the poor man, when he hears of the mangled state in which his wife's body has been found,' Dorothy said.

John said nothing but, though he seemed to have little interest in the sad affair, he knew more about it than he was letting on. He had secrets: some his young wife knew about, others she did not. In fact, he was not John Anderson at all but John Adam. He and Dorothy were not even legally married. In the eyes of the law and the Church, John *was* married – but to another woman. To him it had been a marriage of convenience – his wife had cash and property and he had wanted it. But, as soon as he got it, she became decidedly inconvenient. And now she lay wrapped in preservative cloth in Dingwall Town Hall.

John Adam was born on a farm on Lord Airlie's estate near Forfar on 1 January 1804. He grew up tall and good-looking but he was none too keen on hard work. He had two distinct skills, however – he could charm the ladies and he could lie like a salesman. The Adam family had farmed the Craigieloch holding for three centuries. When John was fourteen, his God-fearing father died and the running of the land was left to him. Unsurprisingly, he showed no ability whatsoever and was soon working at another farm to help pay the family's way.

As the years passed, he grew taller and even more handsome. This attracted the girls and, by the time he was nineteen, he found himself in trouble with the Kirk Session for the seduction of two respectable young women of the parish. The scandal was heightened by the fact that one was not only his cousin but was also deaf and dumb. John Adam had broken hearts left, right and centre but this proved to be the final straw and he was packed off to work on a farm near Brechin. His wandering ways had begun.

At Brechin he met an older woman who, coincidentally, was named Jean Brechin. She was a cook for the family and earned good money. John turned on the charm and she fell for it. There was talk of marriage but only on her part – John was not yet ready to take the plunge. He later said that he could not even look at a younger woman without provoking Jean's jealous rage.

Before long, he took himself off to Aberdeen in search of pastures and conquests new. There he discovered a new circle of friends and the delights of Deism. As the son of a Kirk elder, the young man was unlikely to reject religion totally and Deism accepted the existence of God but not the teachings of the organised Church. This left John and his friends free to ignore the stifling rules and regulations of the Kirk and follow their own path. For John, this path naturally led to the favours of a number of local ladies and it was not long before he was on the road again, fleeing irate fathers and husbands.

He settled for a time in Lanarkshire and here, it seems, he fell in love. This time he proposed marriage and was accepted. The date was set but the wedded bliss the couple hoped for was not to be. One night shortly before they were due to walk down the aisle, John had a series of disturbing dreams. Three times, his bride-to-be appeared beside his bed, her flesh pale and her body swathed in a winding sheet. 'John,' she said sadly each time, 'we shall never be married. My time in this world will be very short. But, mark, you will die an awful death! You and I shall be happy in the world to come.'

The following day, John could not shake off the terror that had gripped him in the night. He decided he had to see his beloved so he obtained time off from his employer and walked to her father's house, arriving just as darkness fell. As he approached the door he heard the sound of hymn singing which was unusual as it was not the Sabbath. He peeped through the window and saw the family clustered around the body of his intended who had died suddenly that morning.

It was time for him to move on again and, this time, he pitched up in Glasgow where he resumed his old ways with the women, both married and single. He also added a few new skills – like robbing his older conquests of their savings. Finally, for reasons best known to himself – perhaps because life was proving somewhat warm for him in Civvy Street – on 7 January 1831 he enlisted in the 2nd Dragoon Guards and eventually found himself in England.

Dorothy Elliot was around twenty when she met the dashing, hazel-eyed Private John Adam. The young man was 6 ft 1 in., handsome and well built. He appeared to be the answer to a maiden's prayer as he strutted about in his uniform. He was, however, quite bald and had taken to wearing a wig. The daughter of Derbyshire miner Edward Elliot, Dorothy was assistant cook in the home of Ralph Ordish, the landlord of the Red Lion Inn in Derby where John Adam was billeted. She took one look at the handsome Scot and, like many others before her, fell for him. It was Christmas Day 1833 when they first met and, by the following March, the romance was burning brightly. By then, John had been moved to the village of Duffield and, one Sunday, Dorothy and the wife of a Sergeant Ramsdale went to visit their men. By the time she got back to Derby, the Ordish house and business were shut up for the night and she could not get back in. Mrs Ordish was affronted that the young girl had stayed out all night and promptly terminated her employment.

Dorothy returned to her father's home in Wirksworth and it was there that John Adam called on her – this time out of uniform. He told her he'd been granted a leave of absence to allow him to return to Scotland and begged her to come with him. She hesitated. He had asked her this before but, because she was a decent girl, she did not wish to go away with a man unless there was a walk down the aisle first. Her family was already unhappy with the relationship so Adam urged her to tell them that they were already wed. He would marry her, he promised, but they could do it on the way.

There was some measure of urgency to his desire to get away from England for he had received no leave of absence from the military. He had, in fact, deserted. This was a serious enough crime without him compounding his felony by making off with sixty pounds in notes and sovereigns.

Dorothy, who obviously loved and trusted John very much, finally agreed to run away with him and the couple caught the mail coach north. But the wedding never took place. John had promised he'd marry her at the first staging post they came to, which was Sheffield, but, when they arrived there, he claimed they did not have enough time. He promised to wed her at York, Edinburgh and Perth but, each time, he made some excuse not to tie the knot. Finally, exhausted by the madcap dash northwards but still single, Dorothy found herself walking five miles to Adam's mother's farm at Craiggieloch which was now managed by John's brother James. They stayed there for about a week and the family, believing the couple to be man and wife, treated Dorothy with great kindness.

John's itchy feet would not let him rest, however. He knew the army would be looking for him, if only to get their money back, and he wanted to move on. He told Dorothy that a local girl with whom he had once had an illegitimate child was pestering him. He had given her some of his money, he explained, but she wanted more. So, to avoid being cleaned out, he felt it was time they took their leave. They left on foot, walking for eight or nine days over the hills, via Braemar and Tomintoul, before arriving in Inverness. Along the way, John confessed to Dorothy that there was more than one bastard child and he would have to adopt a false name to avoid being discovered. Given his reputation, these tales may well have had more than grain of truth in them although he was more likely trying to avoid detection by the authorities. Dorothy, of course, believed everything he said. She was head over heels in love with the handsome Scotsman and clearly would go anywhere and do anything he asked.

Now calling themselves Mr and Mrs John Anderson, the couple lingered a week in Inverness while the remainder of his English notes were exchanged for Scots currency before pressing on to Dingwall where he found a job in a quarry. The work was seasonal, though, and they soon found themselves in financial trouble. It was winter now and, for the young woman, the gilt had worn off the relationship. She missed her family and friends and she was unhappy with the way their life was going. She wanted to be married. John was unwilling to take another step towards the altar and said he did not have the cash to send her home. He only had one pound and he could not spare it. If she would just be patient, he would make everything right. But Dorothy was not to be put off. She had packed her bags and was eager to be away. He pointed out to her that it was winter and the journey home would be hazardous. He suggested that she should wait until the warm weather came and said that, if she would wait until summer, then he would accompany her. She agreed to stay but their funds dropped with the temperature. Finally, John told her he would visit his family and borrow some cash from them.

And so he set off, leaving his young love alone in their Dingwall home. But he was not going to Forfar. He was heading for Montrose – and another woman.

When John Adam reappeared in her life, Jean Brechin was close to fifty years of age – although even her sister was unsure as to her exact age. Jean had worked as a cook for many notable families and had carefully squirrelled her money away to allow her to buy a grocery shop in Montrose. She lived in the back of the premises and had a thriving business. She was not exactly rich but she was comfortably well off. Somehow, John Adam had heard about his former girlfriend's good fortune and this had prompted him to get back in touch with her. During his week away from Dorothy, he paid her a visit, using his old charm and talent for lying to impress her. He was doing very well himself, he said, and told her he was working in Inverness as a lawyer. He said that, over the years, he had often thought of her and what they had once had. If only he had been more mature back then, perhaps things would have been different. He still harboured love for her and would be honoured if she would consider rekindling their old flame.

Jean, described as 'stoutish, plain and ill-favoured', was bowled over. She had almost given up on ever meeting a man with whom she could share her life and her money. Now here was this handsome face from her past, prosperous and wishing to take her hand so that they could spend their lives together in Inverness. Naturally she agreed.

John stayed with her for about a week before returning to the Highlands. After all, he had a practice to tend. The date of their marriage was set for 11 March 1835 and he promised to come back before then to help Jean wind up her affairs in Montrose. In the meantime, if she wished to write to him, she must address her letters care of John Anderson in Dingwall, with whom he was lodging.

And so John Adam returned to the Highlands to become John Anderson again. In March, a letter arrived, the first he had ever received, Dorothy later said. He did not let her read it at first but said it was from his family. He had to return to Forfar, he lied, to claim some money left to him by an uncle who had died in the West Indies. However, Dorothy was no longer so naïve and in love that she believed everything he said. He had never before mentioned an uncle in the West Indies, let alone a relative with money. At any rate, the letter was postmarked 'Montrose'. She caught a glimpse of what it said before John lit his pipe with it and noted that it was 'very ill-written'; the writer said something like 'my mother is very angry with me for working to come north'.

Once again, John Anderson re-adopted his true John Adam persona and travelled south-east. In Montrose, he helped his bride-to-be sell her shop and empty her bank account and also arranged to have her furniture shipped to Dingwall. Then they were married in her mother's village of Laurencekirk. During this time, her brother-in-law had many conversations with him and found him 'of sound mind' and said he 'thought highly of his conversation'.

Now married, John Adam brought his wife to Inverness where he left her in a lodging house while he went off to take care of business. That business involved depositing £100 in the bank account of John Anderson.

When he returned home to Dingwall, Dorothy noticed he had on a new pair of trousers and a waistcoat. He told her his uncle had not left him as much as he had wished but his mother had made up the shortfall by giving him cash left to him by his own father years before. He had other good news for her – an aunt had died, leaving him a considerable amount of good furniture. Clearly, it was open season on the Adam family for his aged relatives seemed to be dropping like flies. There would be a chest of drawers, a trunk, a bed and a box filled with clothes, blankets and pillows. The furniture was on its way and a few days later he went to Inverness to see, he claimed, if it had arrived.

He was indeed awaiting the arrival of furniture but it belonged to Jean Brechin not a deceased aunt. He visited her now and then in the Inverness lodging house in Chapel Street where he had told her she was to stay temporarily. The landlady there noted that the woman read her Bible every night. Jean, though, was becoming restless – she wanted to be in her new home and she wanted her things around her. Her husband told her they would go there as soon as her furniture was delivered. When it finally arrived he put her off, promising to come back for her soon, before setting out for Dingwall in a hired cart with her belongings on the back.

Dorothy greeted the arrival of the much-heralded goods in Dingwall with great pleasure. However, she was puzzled by the initials 'J.B' that were embroidered on some of the linen and clothing. But John had a ready answer – his aunt had once been engaged to marry a man named Burns who had asked her to have his initials sewn into them. Also included in the haul was a selection of scales and weights of the type used in shops.

John Adam now had Jean's money and possessions. The only problem was that he also still had Jean. He was married now – they were legally man and wife. And not until death would they part.

On Monday 30 March 1835, John Adam visited his wife for the last time at her lodgings to tell her that everything was ready. She could leave with him that very night and within a matter of hours they would be together in their new home. They dined on barley broth and then set out in the gathering darkness for Dingwall, Mrs Adam carrying with her an umbrella and a small basket filled with some of her belongings. They arrived at the Kessock ferry that was to carry them across the Beauly Firth to their new life. On the far side the woman thanked the ferryman and followed her husband into the night.

Adam led his wife through the darkness to the ruined cottage at Kilcoy. He'd had murder in mind from the start of their journey and, although this had not been where he'd intended finishing her off, a cacophony of demons clamoured in his brain. 'This is as good a place as any,' they urged. 'It's now or never,' they shrieked. 'Do it NOW! Go on – KILL HER!' they demanded. When she stooped to tie her garter, he seized his chance. Kicking her leg from under her, he pounced on her and pressed his hands over her mouth and nose to cut off her air. She struggled and writhed beneath him, her fingers grasping at his wrists, fists pounding at his chest, legs kicking and jerking beneath his weight. But he held on, tightening his grip until the woman's struggles slowed and weakened and finally stilled. But he was not finished. He turned her over so that she was face down and stamped on her head until blood oozed from her ears. Then he carried her into the cottage and went through her pockets, taking any money, letters and personal items he could find.

But Jean was not yet dead. A small groan escaped from her mouth and, in the moonlight, he could see that her lips were moving slightly. Realising that his bloody work was not yet over, he clamped his hands over her face again but, this time, with such force that he could feel her jaw cracking and breaking. He may also, at some point, have picked up a rock and battered her head with it. Jean's body lay still again but, just in case she was still alive, he pushed the remnants of a stone wall on top of her and made sure she was fully covered with earth and rocks. Perhaps, if she were ever found, it would be thought she had simply been caught under the wall as it fell.

With the demonic choir in his head now silent, he began his long walk home, only to encounter the ghostly figure on the road. The sight so terrified him that he threw the letters and personal items he had stolen from Jean away although he kept the cash, the basket and the umbrella. Ghosts were one thing – valuables were another.

No living person saw him return from the scene of the crime that night although many had seen him in the company of Jean Brechin – too many for his marriage to remain a secret. There was her family, to begin with, as well as the landlady at the Inverness lodging house. Then there was the ferryman who had seen them together. And what about the carter who had transported the furniture to Dingwall? And there was the address he had given Jean – John Adam, care of John Anderson, Dingwall.

On Sunday 13 April – three days after the discovery of the body – the net tightened. John Anderson and his wife Dorothy were awakened in the early hours of the morning by a banging on their door. It was the authorities and they had a warrant for his arrest. He was pulled out of bed, clapped in irons and marched through the streets to the Town House, where his dead wife's body lay as if in state. Witnesses identified him as the man they had seen with the dead woman but he quickly denied this. When he was confronted with the body, he held his hands over his face for an instant, saying he was unused to such sights. The grim-faced men around him had no time for such squeamishness for they suspected it was guilt that made him flinch away. Now they planned to put him under more pressure, namely the Ordeal by Touch. The procurator fiscal told him to lift the left hand of the dead woman. 'Take that hand in your own and say if you know it,' he ordered.

Anderson, his nerve restored, gripped the cold, dead hand and said, 'No, I do not know it.'

The fiscal was not convinced. 'Lay your hand on that face and say if you ever saw that face before. Then place your hand on that bosom and say if your hand was ever there before.'

Anderson did as he was told, swearing, 'I have never seen this woman before – either alive or dead.'

'Very well,' said the fiscal, no doubt disappointed that John had not broken down and confessed, 'we are all in the presence of God who knows best.'

Anderson denied knowing Jean Brechin. He even denied having been in the army. He denied his real name was John Adam, insisting he had been born near Dalkeith and even providing a detailed family history. Either he was incredibly quick-witted or he had been planning this for some time. He said he had actually married Dorothy, described the ceremony and named witnesses. He said he could prove it, for he had a marriage certificate somewhere if only they would let him go to look for it. But the authorities were not taken in by his careful deceit. They knew that, if they gave him an inch, he would take a few hundred miles and put those miles between them and him. They kept him locked up and, probably armed with information provided by the shocked Dorothy, asked the army to send two witnesses to identify him as their deserter. Sergeant James Bleakly and Private Joseph Collier arrived from Ipswich, studied the accused through his cell door and confirmed that he was, indeed, John Adam, deserter and thief.

Within a few weeks the prisoner had changed his tune. Yes, he was John Adam and, yes, he had been in the cavalry and had deserted before bringing poor Dorothy north to Scotland. He admitted marrying Jean but insisted that he did not murder her. She had become tired of the lodging house at Inverness and wanted to leave. He went with her as far as the ferry where he left her at her request. She was to get herself settled, he claimed, and then write to him. That was the last he saw of her.

While he languished in prison awaiting trial, there was some debate over the disposal of Jean Brechin's estate. The question was whether, given John's relationship with Dorothy, the marriage was valid. If it were, what was left of Jean's cash and property would fall to the Crown. If not, it would go to her family. The family was supported in its claim by the minister who had married Jean and John – a curious position for a man of the cloth to take, considering he was suggesting that a lawful marriage was superseded by a sinful relationship. The first suggestion was that the estate should be split between the Crown and the family but, finally, the former gave up its claim because it was decided, as the murder had occurred within a year and a day of the ceremony, that the marriage was officially 'dissolved'.

John Adam, alias John Anderson, faced trial for the murder of Jean Brechin in Inverness on 18 September 1835. Justice in those days was swift for it lasted only two hours and the jury was out for a mere forty minutes before it returned to pronounce him guilty. As the judge donned the black cap and sentenced him to be hanged on Friday 16 October, Adam jumped up and screamed, 'You have condemned an innocent man! I am condemned at the bar of Man but I will not be condemned at the bar of God!' Warders seized and restrained him and, during the struggle, Adam dropped a cut-throat razor which he had hidden. Perhaps he had planned to make an escape bid or perhaps he had intended to cheat the hangman. At any rate, he was taken to Inverness jail where he was kept under constant watch in the condemned cell. Candles were kept burning all night long so that guards could ensure he did not attempt any mischief, prompting a complaint from the prisoner that the light interrupted his sleep.

He continued to profess his innocence, even insisting on it in a letter to Dorothy which, according to some sources, was written in his own blood. The young woman visited him once in jail, on the eve of his execution. She asked him to confess but, even then, he refused. As she left, he advised her to 'beware of bad company' which was somewhat ironic considering the company she had kept for the year between March 1834 and April 1835.

On the eastern shore of the Moray Firth, about a mile from Inverness, the gallows were erected on a site known as the Longman's Grave. Adam had told his jailers that he did not wish to be taken by cart to the rope and 'hung like a dog' but such was the public interest in the case that his hopes of walking his last mile had to be abandoned. Over 8,000 people turned out to see him die. A convoy of three carriages pushed its way through the crowds. Inside one sat Adam, wearing a long black cloak, and the hangman, who had been brought from Ayrshire to do the job, as there was no dedicated executioner in Inverness. The other carriages contained magistrates and local dignitaries. Meanwhile, a small army of 1,100 special constables, sworn in for the day, helped keep the peace. As he climbed to the gallows, Adam gazed across the water to the ridge where he had murdered his wife. Perhaps he felt remorse for the life he had snuffed out. Perhaps he felt sadness for the lives he had tainted with his philandering and thieving ways. And perhaps he felt nothing at all as he turned his back on the view and faced the crowd. A minister suggested he sing the fifty-first psalm but another thought the thirty-first was better. Whatever he felt in his heart, Adam died still claiming he was innocent of the crime.

After the execution, it emerged he had confessed. A fellow prisoner who shared a cell with Adam claimed he had admitted murdering his wife. He had also told him the story of the ghostly figure on the road. That Adam would blurt everything out to a total stranger – and a criminal at that – seems doubtful but not impossible. The ghost story may have merely been a fiction designed to freeze the blood and improve the tale.

The judge had specified that Adam be buried within the precincts of the prison so his body was planted in an upright position beneath a passageway running between the courthouse and the jury room. Why he was interred in a standing position remains a mystery.

He was the last person to be hanged publicly in Inverness. It would be seventy-three years before another convicted murderer met his end in the Highland capital. He was Joseph Hume, who was hanged in 1908 in the recently built Porterfield Prison but, this time, the execution was behind closed doors. Curiously, Hume, found guilty of murdering a man near Elgin, was also an army deserter.

With his 'awful death', Adam had fulfilled the first part of the prophecy made by his dead Lanarkshire lover in his dream all those years ago. Of course, whether he was reunited with her in the world to come cannot be said. Death, however, did not end the man's wandering ways. Some years after his execution, the former prison in Bridge Street was torn down, so his body had to be hauled up and it was reinterred under the front steps of the police office in Castle Wynd. In 1962, that office was also demolished and Adam's remains were on the move again – this time to be buried under the front entrance of the new police office at Farraline Park. In 1975, he was moved again and placed under the police headquarters on Old Perth Road. Still he could not rest. In 1998, Northern Constabulary planned to move to a new headquarters, ironically, very near to the Longman's Grave area where Adam had his date with the hangman.

For many, this was a move too far for the man's remains. There were calls for him to be interred either in the Old High Church graveyard in Chapel Street or back at Castle Wynd where he had first been buried.

There was, however, a problem. The police knew he had been buried under the building in 1975 but no record had been taken of his exact whereabouts. Radar equipment was employed to trace the remains that had been placed in a wooden coffin and then encased in concrete. However, after extensive but fruitless searching, it was decided that Adam's bones would lie in peace this time. In February 1999, the police announced that, after the demolition of the old building was completed, a plaque would be erected to mark the spot of his final resting place and a rose bush was planted in his memory.

After over 160 years, John Adam had finally settled down.

3

THE DEADLY SUITOR

John Thomson

In July 1857, a well-to-do twenty-one-year-old Glasgow girl was on trial for her life. She was charged with poisoning her older French lover by lacing cups of hot chocolate with cyanide. Once she had been passionately in love with him but, earlier that year, he had become tiresome and something of an obstacle to her plans to marry a wealthier and more socially acceptable suitor. She was young, she was beautiful and she was the daughter of a respectable and well-known city architect. She was Madeleine Hamilton Smith.

Her social position, her beauty and the scandalous nature of the case – for it emerged that the seemingly prim Miss Smith had embarked on a wild sexual adventure with the worldly Pierre Emile L'Angelier – made the trial a cause célèbre in the city and beyond. There was nothing the upright and sanctimonious Victorians liked better than a bit of spice. The country was in the middle of an election campaign but the pursuit of political power took second place to the astonishing events unfolding in Glasgow's High Court. The chattering classes could not get enough of the daring revelations while even the lower classes, many of whom had more on their mind than the love lives of the rich and infamous, found themselves discussing the case.

One of those fascinated by the Smith trial was an itinerant tailor then living in the village of Eaglesham, south west of Glasgow. But, for him, it was not the use of cyanide that proved stimulating

– it was the mention of prussic acid during the hearing that set him on the road to murder. He had killed once, many years before, and got away with it. Now he would try again.

And again.

Now a conservation village threatened by the sprawl of East Kilbride, Eaglesham has changed little since 1857. It is bigger, certainly, with more modern houses having sprouted on its outer edges, but its two main streets, linked by a tree-filled grassland, is still very much as it was a century and a half ago. The village, as we know it, was created in the eighteenth century by the Earls of Eglinton, who also built a cotton-spinning mill that was powered by the small stream that runs through the central green. Later, in 1826, the mill grew in size as two dams above the village helped to provide more water power. The mill burned down in 1876 – but that was after the events that saw one of its workers die an agonising death.

Agnes Montgomery, a twenty-seven-year-old reeler, lived halfway up one of the two main streets, on the upper floor of a two-storey house. She was unmarried but she was never lonely for many of her family lived nearby. In fact, her sister Janet and her husband James Watson, a tailor, occupied one of the flats on the ground floor of Agnes's building. In September 1857, the Watsons had a lodger, John Thomson, a twenty-six-year-old tailor who had come to work for James that June. He told his employer that he belonged to Dundee and had recently been working in Glasgow. He seemed a capable enough worker but there was something about him that they did not trust. What didn't help was a letter from an Archibald Mason of John Street in Glasgow, with whom Thomson lodged whenever he was in Glasgow. Mr Mason said that the young tailor was suspected of stealing clothing from another of his guests.

Like John Adam before him, John Thomson was a man of many secrets. His name, for starters, was actually Peter Walker and he was from Tarbert, in Argyll, not Dundee. And he had not been working in Glasgow. He was a ticket-of-leave prisoner who had been released on licence, in June the previous year, from Woolwich Prison. There, he had been serving seven years' transportation from Scotland, after being sentenced for theft at Inveraray Court, in April 1853. 'Had we known he was such,' said Janet Watson later, 'he would not have had another hour in our home.'

Unfortunately, they had no idea he was a convicted felon until it was too late. It was especially unfortunate for Agnes Montgomery who, unknown to her family, became more than friendly with the sticky-fingered lodger downstairs. In addition to a lack of regard for other people's property, women were Thomson's downfall – just as Thomson would be Agnes's. His conviction for theft followed a fling with his boss's daughter during which, in order to impress her, he overspent. Finding himself in debt, he decided the only thing to do was to break into the premises of his employer James Bell, Tailors and Clothiers, in Lochgilphead, Argyll, and help himself to some £22 in cash and articles of clothing.

That was not the only amorous scrape he enjoyed while living at Lochgilphead. His landlord, Peter Fletcher, later said, 'He was particularly artful, cunning and deceiving and aggravated me in a private matter that I don't wish to mention.' He went on, 'He is very insidious and flattering and it is difficult to find him out. He can state a lie with the utmost confidence and is quite qualified to veil any intentions he may have.' Clearly, Thomson, or Walker as he was known there, had upset his former landlord somehow.

Mr Fletcher's wife Christina believed that Thomson had a habit of associating too much with girls who flirted after him and 'on that account I thought him foolish and he had a habit of telling untruths,' she said. She also said that her husband was 'sometimes a little nervous and weak in mind' and she added, 'He has a prejudice against the prisoner and is affected with a delusion that I wish to take my husband's life and take the prisoner as a husband instead.' It seems then that young Mister Walker had been taking the idea of bed and breakfast a little too far where his landlady was concerned.

It is unclear just when he and Agnes Montgomery began their ill-fated affair. Her sister said there was nothing between them but fellow mill-worker Mary Donald saw them together at Dollar's Pub in the village. Thomson had his arm on Agnes's shoulder and the witness could see there was obvious affection between them. Mary told Agnes that she would not deny it the next day, meaning she planned to tell their co-workers at the mill, and Agnes merely laughed in reply.

Thomson was much taken with Agnes and asked her to come away with him to Glasgow. Agnes, though, was not as smitten so she refused. She had a life in Eaglesham, she had family and she had no intention of moving to the city with a penniless tailor. Despite being seen with him, she still refused to acknowledge to her sister that there was something between them. She did not treat him seriously at all – on one occasion she and her friend Janet Dollar, whose family owned the pub, threw water over him as a joke. Thomson did not take this treatment well. He went back to his room soaking wet, telling Janet Watson, 'Those buggers upstairs did it and I'll give it to them.'

Local weaver George King said that Thomson was easily offended over trifling matters. He recalled once being in the Cross Keys bar room with Thomson who said, 'I'll tell you what it is, King, there is a lot of them has me at ill will but I am determined to do for the buggers yet.' A few days later, the weaver had cause to remember that statement.

At around 5.20 p.m. on Sunday 13 September, Janet Watson was standing in the close of her home talking with neighbour Mrs McDonald when they heard a strange moaning coming from upstairs. Janet said it was probably one of their other neighbours who had been complaining of stomach problems. The groans, though, were coming from Agnes's flat and Janet knew this as soon as she went inside. She and Mrs McDonald dashed up the stairs and they found another concerned neighbour standing in front of Agnes's door which had been locked from the outside.

They managed to spring the lock with a coal cellar key and went inside. Agnes was sitting on a chair, her head resting on the table beside it. Janet cradled her sister's head and saw her eyes were wide and staring while a trickle of blood-flecked saliva drooled from her mouth. A tumbler sat on the table and Janet saw there was whitish sediment on the bottom. 'Oh, Aggie, have you taken anything?' Janet asked. She had seen her less than an hour before and she had been in perfect health. Now Agnes could neither speak nor move. All she could do was give 'a strange moan', said Janet, and retch a few times as if she was trying to vomit. When nothing came up Janet tried making her sick by pushing her fingers down her throat but a sudden paroxysm brought the dying woman's teeth slicing into her flesh. Their Uncle Hugh also lived in the house and he cut open the lace of his niece's stays to give her some air. Then spinner William Muir and baker James Fulton, who had been out in the street, came up to see what was going on. Hugh Montgomery noticed that the fingers of Agnes's right hand were badly cramped and he suggested they bathe them. The stiff fingers responded to the warm water but never fully eased.

John Thomson, who had been with the two men in the street, fetched local GP, Dr Scott, who said they should move her into bed and Thomson readily agreed, throwing off his coat and preparing to help. A look from Janet convinced Muir and Fulton that Thomson was not wanted here and they ushered him away. Dr Scott said they should give the woman a toddy but Janet could not say if any of it was swallowed. Agnes was sighing heavily by this time and was totally unconscious. She remained in that condition for another forty-five minutes before she died.

Both Janet and Dr Scott had thought at first that the dead woman had taken something that caused her death. Mrs McDonald had smelt something strange as soon as she had entered Agnes's house. Another neighbour, slater and mole-catcher David Clarkson, had earlier heard a loud crash come from the house and, when he looked out, he had seen John Thomson leaving. He suspected nothing sinister but merely thought the man had thrown the woman down during some horseplay, suggesting that such devilment between the two of them was nothing unusual. However, Mr Clarkson did note that this was strange conduct for a Sunday. Thomson's friends, Muir and Fulton, had heard the groans coming from upstairs but thought Agnes had a drunk man in there. When Thomson came out to meet them, they mentioned this to him but all he did was laugh.

Few questions were asked about Agnes Montgomery's death and she was buried in Eaglesham Churchyard on September 17. Doubts, however, remained. It was known John Thomson had been the last person to see the woman alive and he had been acting very strangely since her death. Whenever it was mentioned, he hung his head and refused to respond. James Watson said he began to think Thomson had something to do with the sudden death but said his wife 'would not credit it'.

Prior to burial, the body lay out in a room and Thomson was among those who came to pay their respects. Marion Young, another of Agnes's sisters, noticed he did not get too close to the coffin but chose to keep his distance. However, he could not take his eyes off the dead woman's face. 'You would be the last that spoke to her in this world,' Marion said to him and he agreed that he was. Then he finally turned away from the body.

Although he was at the gathering afterwards, Thomson was not among the mourners at the funeral. Marion Young handed him a glass of sherry and told him it was in remembrance of Aggie. He grudgingly took the drink and, with his eyes fixed firmly on the floor, drained the glass before leaving.

None of this was conclusive proof, of course, that John Thomson had anything to do with Aggie's abrupt passing – but it was enough to make the already suspicious James Watson think things over. He recalled many conversations about the Madeleine Smith case between Thomson, himself and John, his brother. John was a wood carver to trade but he had recently turned to the new art of photography to make a living. Thomson believed the Glasgow woman deserved to hang for what she had done but John Watson thought she had been 'sufficiently punished by the exposure of a person in her station [of life]'. But what really stuck in the mind was a conversation about poison. News reports of the trial stated that L'Angelier had been killed by arsenic poisoning and, at one point, Miss Smith had sent a boy for sixpence worth of the prussic acid. Thomson had wondered what sort of substance it was and James Watson later recalled, 'I said it was the kind of stuff that, if she had got it and had given sixpence-worth of it to L'Angelier, she could not have got out of his company till he was dead.' – meaning that just sixpence-worth of the poison would have been enough to kill a person almost instantaneously.

L'Angelier had managed to stagger from Miss Smith's home to his own lodgings before he died. This prompted John Watson to opine that 'prussic acid would never have done for the man would have died instantly', adding that 'even though the acid was diluted, the man would never have made it home'. Thomson wondered where it could be obtained and was told it was readily available at the apothecary. Photographers used it in their business, he was told, although John Watson preferred to use potassium cyanide. Poison was obviously in Thomson's mind but, with the Smith case being on almost everyone's lips, that was hardly damning.

In Agnes's house, sediment had been seen in a tumbler on the table but that had been cleaned and put away. And a bottle of beer, also seen in the premises, was also long gone. By 25 September so was Thomson. He would have been aware of the dark suspicions that were haunting his life in Eaglesham and must have decided it was time to move on. If he had got away with murder, the prudent course would be to quit while he was ahead. And so, taking an envelope containing one pound from his employer's house – for old habits die hard – he headed into Glasgow where he hoped to lose himself.

But murder, he found, can be habit forming.

At about 11 p.m. on 25 September, sixty-five-year-old Archibald Mason was awakened in his bed by Thomson. 'Father,' said the younger man in his accustomed way, 'will you have a dram?' He proffered a pint bottle of what he said was 'good Paisley whisky'. Mr Mason politely agreed to take a drink but passed the glass back, saying it had a strange taste and brought a flush to his face. He hadn't particularly wanted a drink anyway. Thomson then handed the glass to Mason's wife who was in bed beside her husband. She downed about half of it before she complained that it had a curious taste and asked if it had bitters in it.

Thomson shook his head, saying, 'No, it's the best spirits.' And offered her some more. However, Mrs Mason had had enough so the glass was laid on the chest of drawers while the bottle was corked and returned to Thomson's pocket. Curiously, at no stage, had he attempted to take a drink. He sat in the chair talking to Mr Mason while Mrs Mason went downstairs to the kitchen. When she came back, she told them she had taken violently ill downstairs and had to crawl back up on her hands and knees. She said she'd felt 'very dizzy and stupid' and believed there was something wrong with the whisky. Thomson insisted again that it was the very best whisky.

He asked if he could stay the night and, although they had no bed to spare, the Masons agreed. He was suspected of not only stealing a previous tenant's clothes but also a Bible and brush from them. They wanted to keep him there until they could alert the police, so he was allowed to sleep in the bed with Mr Mason while his wife slept in the kitchen. Mrs Mason was ill throughout the night and her husband was convinced that something was badly wrong with the whisky. The following morning, while Thomson was still asleep, he took the bottle from his pocket and poured the remainder of the whisky from the glass into a phial. Mason then went to the police and told them that Thomson was in the house. Next, he went to a doctor and asked for something he could give to his sick wife. He showed the bottle to the doctor who said it was filled with methylated spirits. The doctor then gave him a powder to be administered to Mrs Mason and a mustard poultice to be placed on her stomach.

By the time Mr Mason returned home, Thomson had been arrested for the theft of the clothes, the Bible and the brush. He was remanded in custody for a time but, as there was insufficient evidence to merit any further prosecution, he was released. He savoured his new-found freedom for only a few minutes before being arrested again – this time it was for the first murder and attempted murder by prussic acid recorded in Scottish criminal history.

James Watson had reported the theft of the pound note to Constable Robert McLaurin of the Renfrewshire County force. To the policeman's surprise, he was also told that Thomson, the person Watson suspected of the theft, might also have poisoned Agnes Montgomery. The officer duly had Mr and Mrs Watson taken to the Paisley procurator fiscal who was then attending the circuit court in Glasgow. They repeated their allegations and it was decided that Thomson should be brought in for questioning. It was very quickly ascertained that Thomson had been in custody on the theft charge but had just recently been liberated.

He was still in the courthouse and, by chance, the Watsons spotted him standing at the witness gate. When Detective Officer Alexander Cushing told him he was being arrested for the murder of Agnes Montgomery, he replied, 'Good God, don't mention that here.' He drew the officer aside and said, 'You'll surely not bring that against me.' But bring that against him they did.

As soon as the investigation became official, further bricks were laid in the wall of evidence against him. A carrier's boy, John Ferguson, said Thomson had sent him to a Glasgow druggist to fetch sixpence worth of prussic acid, having been instructed to say it was for a portrait painter. On the day Agnes died, another villager recalled seeing Thomson walking across the village green, on his way to call the doctor, and watched as he stooped at a tree. A search around the tree later uncovered the missing key to Agnes's door.

But most telling of all was Janet Watson's daughter, also named Janet, who was the only eyewitness to the actual murder. But at only three years of age, her testimony had to be viewed with some suspicion.

She said she had been in her Auntie Aggie's house when Jack, as she knew Thomson, came in and gave her aunt what she referred to as 'some ginger'. Ginger is a Scottish word for lemonade or any other soft drink but it was actually beer that had contained the poison. The taste of the beer would easily have masked the presence of the prussic acid. The wee girl then said that her Auntie Aggie 'spewed' and fell on the floor after drinking from the tumbler. Jack helped Aggie up into the chair and then took the child out and, in the garden at the back of the house, she watched as he put a tiny glass bottle down on the ground and smashed it with his heel. Later, he bought the child's silence with some sweets. But the child could not keep silent, especially after continual questioning from her parents. She had been loath to say anything, crying, 'I'm no' to tell for Jack is to give me a bawbee [a Scots coin of low value].'

For his part, Thomson admitted being in the house with the child but he said Agnes was perfectly healthy when they left and was breaking up sticks for the fire. He denied giving Agnes beer and further denied sending Ferguson to fetch prussic acid although he told police officers he did use the substance as a hair dye. He recalled that he had once sent the lad to fetch him some lavender water and balsam but never prussic acid.

But someone had given Agnes Montgomery prussic acid. Once murder had been alleged and Thomson arrested, the body was exhumed from Eaglesham Kirkyard and was handed over to doctors for examination. But the body had been in the ground for almost three weeks and was bloated with gases and greatly decomposed. There were no wounds but the face was much disfigured and very dark, nearly black, in colour. The swollen tongue protruded between the front teeth while the eyeballs, the corneas quite opaque, bulged from their sockets. The skin was a greenish-yellow colour and greasy to the touch. The fingers of the right hand were firmly bent inward.

When the stomach was opened, the doctors detected the smell of bitter almonds and this suggested death by poisoning. But, even though they could confirm that death was not caused by injury or illness and had actually found minute traces of hydrocyanic acid – more commonly called prussic acid – the authorities could not be certain it had killed her until a proper chemical analysis was carried out. For this, they would need an expert.

On 6 October 1857, the Paisley procurator fiscal sent Superintendent Hunter of Renfrew County Police to the Crown Office with a letter and a tin box filled with certain items. The letter read:

> . . . from the nature of the substance alleged to have been administered, as well as from the state of decomposition in which the body was found, it will be proper that an analysis should be made by some properly qualified person in Edinburgh, accustomed to such matters. I have accordingly, by direction of the sheriff, caused a portion of the stomach and other parts of the body brought away to be sealed up in a jar by Dr McKinlay, in whose custody they have remained since the body was raised, and I now send them by the Bearer, Mr Hunter, superintendent of our County Police, enclosed in a tin box, soldered up in his presence, that you may have the goodness to give directions for them to be placed in the hands of the person usually employed for the Crown in such cases in Edinburgh for analysis, I have directed the bearer to await your directions and to place the Box with its contents in the hands of such person personally . . .

Inside the tin box, sealed in airtight glass jars, were one half of the stomach, a portion of the right lobe of liver, one half of the heart, one half of the spleen, one half of a kidney and portions of the duodenum, ileum, colon and rectum. The stomach, though much distended by flatus, contained neither solid nor liquid matter. And the heart and large blood vessels contained no blood.

The man who ultimately received Superintendent Hunter's grisly cargo was Dr Douglas McLaglan and it was the lack of blood in the majority of the samples that caused him problems. After his initial tests proved negative for poisons, he commented:

> It is in no respect surprising to me that I did not obtain better results even had I been assured otherwise that Agnes Montgomery must have swallowed prussic acid; for besides the well known difficulty of finding this very volatile poison in bodies dead for some time I must observe that I have seldom in the course of my experience met with articles less fitted for medico-legal purposes than those which I have had to operate on.

However, the prosecutors were not to be deterred and, after some insistence from the Crown Office, Dr McLagan reluctantly agreed to have another try. This time, thanks to the blood in the spleen, he found 'unequivocal proof of the presence of prussic acid'. Traces of the poison were also found in the pint bottle from which Thomson had poured the whisky in the Mason murder attempt. However, there was none on fragments of glass found by James Watson in the garden after his daughter had said she had seen Jack stamp on a small bottle there. Thomson had claimed he used prussic acid as hair dye so samples of his hair and beard had been snipped while he was in prison. However, Dr Daniel Mckinlay stated that he had found the samples uniform in colour from root to point. The whiskers were jet black and the hair very dark brown, approaching black. The doctor applied prussic acid to the samples but said it made no difference to colour.

And so, on 22 December, John Thomson came to trial and, although the prosecution could produce no clear motive for the murder of Agnes Montgomery or the attempted murder of Mr and Mrs Mason, it would prove to be a black Christmas for him. On 24 December, after being absent from the courtroom for just ten minutes, the jury returned a guilty verdict. Thomson was to hang on 14 January 1858. Unusually, there was no attempt to obtain a commutation of sentence.

The case had excited public attention and it was estimated that around 20,000 people thronged the streets of Paisley for the execution – a large number of them women and young girls, it was noted somewhat disapprovingly by one reporter. The crowd was, by and large, well behaved. The *Glasgow Herald* noted that 'there was but little noise and almost an entire absence of the disgusting sights that are too frequently to be seen around a gallows tree'. The gallows were erected outside the County Buildings, much to Thomson's discomfort. He had apparently shown remorse over his crimes after sentence but had refused to see any of his relatives. He had requested that he should be hanged in prison but this was refused. He would face the public and the public would see him dangle.

Although he had appeared faint on the morning of his execution, Thomson went to his death in a composed manner. He had requested that no clergy attend him. This was something of a break in tradition for condemned men but there were three ministers on hand should he change his mind. When hangman William Calcraft loosed the trap and Thomson's body fell, a number of men and women close to the scaffold fainted with fright. His body hung for half an hour before being taken down 'in such a brisk and disgusting way as to cause loud shouts of disapprobation from the crowd'. As the *Glasgow Herald* again reported, instead of being lowered down, the cord around the neck was merely loosened and the hangman's assistant 'in the most revolting way, carried it, head and legs together, off the scaffold'.

Thomson's was the ninth execution in Paisley since 1700. Earlier hangings had taken place at Gallow's Green, where George Street crossed Maxwellton Street. One of the men who had met their end at the hangman's noose had been sentenced to death for nothing more than the theft of some green kale. However, another, Alexander Provan, had murdered his wife and was not only hanged but also had his right hand struck off. The last execution before Thomson had been that of William Pirrie in October 1837. During a fit of jealousy, he had murdered his wife in a frenzied attack with a three-edged file. Prior to the attack, he had taken the precaution of locking their children out of the house.

So why had John Thomson killed Agnes Montgomery? Was it because she had spurned his offer of going away together? Was he more interested in her than she with him? Was he so obsessed with her that he decided that if he could not have her then no one else would? Or was he punishing her for something that no one else knew about? Thomson himself remained silent about his crimes apart from a brief comment he reportedly made in prison. He said he had no option but to commit murder – that he was 'impelled to the commission of crimes through an influence for which he could not account'.

It transpired that whatever demons had forced him to poison Agnes Montgomery and attempt to kill the Masons had lain dormant in him for seventeen years. Prior to his execution, he confessed to another murder that he committed at the age of just nine when he was growing up near Tarbert. He said he had pushed another young boy into a quarry hole and drowned him. And, as he swung on the end of that rope before the Paisley crowd, perhaps he saw the creatures that tormented him fly off in search of fresh victims. Human nature being what it is, they would not have had very far to look for candidates.

4

DO NO HARM

Dr Edward Pritchard

She was not dead, he said, only in a faint.

She was not dead, he said, but only needed some hot water to restore the heat to her body.

She was not dead, he said, for he was a doctor and he knew these things.

But she was dead, her body already cooling as it lay on their bed, what little colour there had been draining from her pale flesh. The two servants standing uselessly at the bedside knew this – and so did the tall bearded man who knelt at his wife's side, her lifeless hand in his.

'Is she dead, Patterson?' the doctor asked his cook, the elder of the two women.

'You should know, doctor, better than I,' she replied.

And then the tears came and he cried out to the corpse, 'Come back, come back, my dear Mary Jane! Don't leave your dear Edward!' Then he said, 'What a brute! What a heathen!' and asked one of the servants to fetch a rifle and shoot him.

But they did not for one of them felt the man was merely grief-stricken. It had, after all, been a difficult year. His beloved mother-in-law had been taken from them suddenly, not three weeks before, and now his wife had finally succumbed to whatever malady had been attacking her for some months. He had every right to be overly demonstrative. But the other servant knew more. She knew he was not as devoted a husband as he appeared on this dark March night. For she had been his lover at least since the summer before. He had made her pregnant. He had promised marriage if his wife died. And now, here his wife was, lying dead in their matrimonial bed. The question in the young servant's mind now was, 'Would he keep his promise?'

Perhaps he would have – but there was no new wife ahead of Dr Edward Pritchard. All that was in his immediate future was arrest, prison, a celebrated trial and an agonising death in front of 100,000 jeering spectators.

Edward William Pritchard first met Mary Jane Taylor in Portsmouth in 1850. She was the daughter of a wealthy Edinburgh silk merchant and he was a young doctor with the Royal Navy, then serving on *HMS Hecate*. There had been very little doubt that the boy Pritchard would serve with the navy, even though he showed an early interest in the medical profession. His father was a sea captain, two of his uncles were admirals and two brothers also served with the Senior Service, one as a surgeon. So young Edward merged the two ambitions. By the age of twenty-one, Edward was on board *HMS Victory* – which, in a former life, was Lord Horatio Nelson's flagship – serving as assistant surgeon. In the same year, 1846, he became a member of the Royal College of Surgeons. During the next four years he sailed the seas on Her Majesty's Service, serving in the Pacific, Mediterranean and the Atlantic.

It was while the *Hecate* was home on leave that the dashing young officer attended a ball and met the future Mrs Pritchard. Mary Jane was visiting her uncle, a retired naval surgeon and, at the ball, she was introduced to the striking young doctor who looked so handsome in his uniform – especially as his skin was burnished by foreign suns. They met, they fell in love and Pritchard proposed. With the full approval of her family, they were married that autumn. However, they did not have long to enjoy married life for the new bridegroom was still a serving officer and subject to the call of duty. Soon he was off on the *Hecate* again, braving the wind and the foam for Queen and Country, while his wife went home to her mother and father in Edinburgh.

In March 1851, Pritchard resigned from the navy and set himself up in medical practice at Hunmanby and Filey in Yorkshire where he remained for six years. There, he published books on local subjects and submitted articles to medical journals but, it would appear, he also built himself a reputation for self-publicity and wandering hands. He became a Freemason and used his position there to further his own ends. He even had himself photographed in the official Freemason robes and had them made into calling cards handed out liberally. His love of himself was exceeded only by his love of women and there are suggestions that he was capable of more than a medical inspection when confronted with a pretty patient. During his six years in Yorkshire, he made few friends and, when he left the area under a cloud of debt and amid a storm of gossip, no one, it seems, was sorry to see the back of him.

In 1857, he purchased a Doctor of Medicine diploma from the University of Erlangen in Germany and, two years later, set off for Egypt and the Holy Land as a private medical aide to a well-set-up gentleman. There was, however, no desert sun for poor Mary Jane, who returned to the cold winds of Edinburgh for a year.

Finally, in 1860, the wanderer returned to set up home and a new practice in Glasgow. Moving into their new house at 11, Berkeley Terrace was to mark a new beginning for the Pritchard family. Now with young children, perhaps he could put his restless ways behind him and build a future for them all. But Pritchard, who had been described by one Yorkshire acquaintance as the 'prettiest liar' who spoke the truth only by accident, was too much of a con man to change now. He exaggerated his medical prowess, forged letters of introduction and reference and generally so alienated the city's medical establishment that they wished to have nothing to do with him. His attempts to join medical bodies and societies were met with failure. But you cannot keep a bad man down and Pritchard, exuding bonhomie and charm, took a new approach to garner popularity. If he could not win the stuffy pill-pushers and sawbones over, then he would appeal to the city's artistic nature. He had, after all, already proved himself a Man of Letters with his books on Filey and about his travels to the Pitcairn Islands. He joined artistic societies, became director of the Glasgow Athenaeum and discovered a new skill as lecturer, amazing a rapt audience with descriptions of his travels across the globe. That he was well travelled cannot be denied but, even at the time, it was noted that his tales grew with the telling and he often gave differing accounts of the same journey.

His public esteem was significantly increased by his claim that he was personally acquainted with General Garibaldi – and he had a walking stick supposedly inscribed by the Liberator of Italy to prove it. But this particular claim really took the biscuit with the cognoscenti, for the inscription had been made on his own orders and the closest he ever got to Garibaldi was knowing the man's name.

Despite Pritchard's attempts to better his social standing, it became evident that you cannot always teach an old doctor new tricks. In the Empire's Second City, he joined a number of Masonic Lodges, including the Knights Templar of the Glasgow Priory and the Lodge of St Mark, of which he became Master. But, just as in Yorkshire, his enthusiasm for the Craft stemmed from self-aggrandisement and the social connections such a membership afforded. He still thought highly of himself – he continued to have photographs taken for printing on calling cards – but, although his practice was busy enough, he never won the hearts or minds of his fellow medicos.

However it was in Glasgow he did learn one new skill. For it was here he may have become a killer for the first time.

At around 3 a.m. on 5 May 1863, a police constable, walking his beat in Berkeley Terrace, in the city's west end, saw smoke billowing from the top floor of a house on the north side of the street. He rushed across the road and rang the doorbell. The door was opened quickly by Dr Pritchard, who explained his sons, who had been alerted by smell of smoke and the sound of breaking glass, had already awakened him. His children were safe, he said, and his wife was away from home for the night, but his serving girl, Elizabeth McGirn, could not be roused from her attic room, which seemed to be source of the blaze. The police officer tried to fight his way in but the flames had taken hold of the top part of the house by that time and so he rushed to Anderston police station to raise the alarm. The Central Fire Brigade station was contacted by telegraph, firefighters were soon on the scene and the blaze efficiently tackled.

Elizabeth McGirn was, of course, dead – her charred body being found on her bed. She lay on her back with her left arm by her side and what was left of her right bent outwards. However, the arm from hand to elbow had been almost entirely consumed. Her head was blackened and the flesh of her chest burned away to reveal her ribcage. Her toes were charred but her legs, presumably protected by the blankets, were relatively unmarked.

The fire, it was ascertained, had broken out at the top of the bed, presumably because she had left the gas jet on after falling asleep while reading, although the book must have been totally destroyed by the flames. The bed hangings ignited and the flames spread throughout the room and thereafter to the entire top floor.

But the question as to why had she not tried to escape remained. The position of the body showed no sign of her having panicked or even having been aware of the blazing room. The door was only a few feet away but she lay on the bed as if she were asleep. It was suggested that she had been suffocated by smoke while she slept but was it likely that she would have been overcome so quickly by smoke that she did not make any attempt at all to escape? Or was she already dead when the fire started? Or at least drugged?

Rumours soon circulated that there was more between Dr Pritchard and the unfortunate girl than a simple master–servant relationship. It was hinted that the girl was pregnant but this was not confirmed at the post-mortem. Pritchard was put to some questioning but no further action was taken although he did have a spot of trouble claiming the insurance money regarding the damage to his house. However, after a bit of legal wrangling, a settlement figure was reached and, in the spring of 1864, the family were once again on the move. This time, however, they did not have far to go – just around the corner really, first to Royal Crescent and then to a new house in Clarence Place, Sauchiehall Street.

Whether Pritchard murdered Elizabeth McGirn after getting her pregnant or just to keep her quiet when his incessant womanising threatened to get him into trouble, we will never know. But it was in Clarence Place that his talent for murder really took hold.

At first, Mary Jane Pritchard thought she had merely caught a chill or, at worst, a dose of influenza. She developed headaches and was often sick and her subsequent depressions forced her to take to her bed. However, up until that time, her constitution had been far from delicate. As William Roughead, the doyen of Scottish crime writers, pointed out, she was a robust woman of thirty-eight who had given birth to five children in fifteen years and had put up with the various 'vicissitudes incidental to . . . matrimony with her unconventional consort'.

Her sickness first manifested itself in October 1864 and, the following month, against her husband's wishes, she went to Edinburgh to stay for a time with her mother, Jane Taylor. Once there, Mary Jane's health improved greatly. Her colour returned, she put on weight and she was soon back to her old self. By Christmas, she was thought well enough to return to her Glasgow home and once again shoulder her wifely duties.

But she should have stayed in Edinburgh for, within two weeks of her arriving back at Clarence Place, her illness returned – with a vengeance. She could not keep food or liquid down and soon all the weight she had gained while staying with her mother had dropped away. Catherine Lattimer, the cook, heard her throwing up in the pantry and on being summoned to Mrs Pritchard's

bedroom found her in agony from cramps in her stomach and
sides. Her hands were also affected – during the attacks, the fingers
became stiff and straight and the thumb was twisted underneath.
'Catherine,' said the seriously ill woman, 'I have lost my senses. I
never was as bad as this before.

Dr Pritchard arrived and gave his wife some spirits and water
but the symptoms continued for some time afterwards. On the
surface at least, her husband appeared deeply concerned by his
wife's condition. He contacted her cousin Dr James Cowan, also a
doctor, and asked him to come to Glasgow and offer a second
opinion. Pritchard said his wife was suffering from irritation of the
stomach so Dr Cowan suggested that a mustard poultice be applied.
He also prescribed small quantities of champagne. Once back home
in Edinburgh, Dr Cowan contacted Mrs Taylor and suggested she
go to Glasgow to relieve some of the household pressures on her
daughter. There were only two servants and with a husband and
four children to look after – at the time, the eldest daughter, Fanny,
was staying with her maternal grandparents – things could not be
easy.

Meanwhile, Mary Jane's condition was worsening. As her
husband stood over her, the cook, Catherine Lattimer, heard Mary
Jane say to him, 'Don't cry. If you cry, you are a hypocrite.' Catherine
Lattimer looked but saw no tears in the doctor's eyes. As the
ferocious stomach cramps struck her again, she demanded to see
Dr William Gairdner, a noted physician who was resident in nearby
Blythswood Square. Dr Gairdner, Professor of Medicine at the
University of Glasgow, duly attended and was told by Dr Pritchard
that his wife was suffering from catalepsy. Later, at the trial, Dr
Gairdner would testify that Pritchard's diagnostic skills were 'a
little at random' and that he was not 'a model of accuracy, wisdom
and caution in applying names to things'. Mrs Pritchard, Dr
Gairdner noted, was somewhat the worse for drink and Pritchard
was forced to admit he had been giving her spirits on the advice
of Dr Cowan. Dr Gairdner ordered him to stop giving the woman
strong drink and promised to return the following day. When he

did so, he found the patient much improved. While the two men conferred by the fire, Mrs Pritchard was heard to say, 'You are hypocrites together.' That was Dr Gairdner's last visit to the Pritchard household. He did, however, write to Mary Jane's brother, also a doctor, who had a practice in Penrith, and expressed a wish that she should lodge with him for a time. But Dr Pritchard said his wife was not well enough to travel. This was probably true but it was not his real reason for wishing to keep her at home.

And then Mrs Taylor arrived to take charge. The seventy-year-old woman, alarmed by Dr Cowan's description of her daughter's condition, had rushed from Edinburgh to help. She immediately took over everything to do with Mary Jane's wellbeing. She supervised her eating habits. She even slept in the same room so that she was available day and night. She wanted her daughter well again so that she could take care of her husband and her family once more. Mrs Taylor was a kind and considerate Victorian lady.

But she was in the way now.

On Monday 13 February, three days after her mother arrived to care for her, Mary Jane Pritchard decided she would like some tapioca. The fact that she was showing interest at all in food was a good thing so one of the children was sent to fetch some. The packet lay unattended on a table in the hall before it was taken into the kitchen. Half a cup full was prepared by Catherine Lattimer and taken upstairs to Mrs Pritchard's room. Mary Jane only had a taste of the pudding, telling Catherine Lattimer that it was not very good and it was rather tasteless. However, Mrs Taylor ate the tapioca. The vomiting began almost immediately and she thought that she had developed a touch of whatever ailed her daughter. She could not have been more right.

Eleven days later she was dead. By that time, Catherine Lattimer had left the household to take up another position but she often returned to visit the children and talk to Mrs Taylor. On 24 February, she spoke to the older woman who was still puzzled by her daughter's condition. 'I don't understand her illness,' she said. 'She is one day better and two worse.'

That night, servants Mary Patterson, who had replaced Catherine Lattimer as cook, and sixteen-year-old maid Mary McLeod found Mrs Taylor in the bedroom. She was sitting in an armchair, unable to move but gagging and retching. Her daughter sat in the bed, calling to her, 'Mother, dear mother, can you not speak to me?' Dr Pritchard was called and, as they moved the woman on to the bed, a small bottle fell from her dress which Mary Patterson recognised as Battley's Sedative Solution, an opium-based drug which the woman used to combat severe headaches. Pritchard grabbed the bottle and, seeing it was half-empty, remarked, 'Good heavens – has she taken this much since Tuesday?'

He immediately sent for another medical man, Dr James Paterson – and so began one of the most puzzling aspects of the case. For this doctor had it in his power to save Mrs Pritchard but chose, for whatever reason, not to do anything. There was, however, nothing he could do to save poor Mrs Taylor. Pritchard had told him she had suffered an apoplectic fit but Dr Paterson knew that was not the case. It had also been hinted that she was addicted to laudanum but the cause of the elderly lady's illness was not an overdose of opium. 'If a person is in the habit of taking opium to a great extent,' he said in evidence, 'you generally find that they are not very good in colour. They are generally thin in features and hollow about the eyes – in fact, not of a healthy appearance generally.' Mrs Taylor, he noted, was stout and healthy looking. He knew immediately, though, that she was under the influence of some drug – but not opium.

As he had examined Mrs Taylor, he could not help but notice her daughter who was sitting up in bed and obviously in a very distressed state. She was ill, he knew that, and by her appearance – and her mother's – he felt someone in this house was administering poison. More specifically, he suspected antimony. It is believed the ancient Egyptians discovered the poisonous qualities of antimony but, as usual, it was the Romans who used it to great effect, as an emetic. Revellers would eat and drink their fill, swallow some antimony and immediately vomit, thus clearing some space to continue with the feasting and imbibing. However, in small doses administered over a period of time, the substance is lethal. The victim suffers violent cramps, continuous vomiting, chronic diarrhoea, extreme weakness and depression. Violent cramp attacks the limbs and, towards the end, the skin can turn cyanotic or blue. Dr Paterson was a good enough physician to spot the signs in both women but, amazingly, despite his strong suspicions, he said nothing. He tried to rouse Mrs Taylor and was rewarded by a brief moment of consciousness, during which the ever-solicitous Pritchard said to his mother-in-law, 'You are getting better, darling.'

But Dr Paterson knew better. 'Never in this world,' he muttered.

Announcing there was nothing he could do, Dr Paterson left. At just before 1 a.m. the following morning, he was asked to return but refused, believing it was only a matter of time before the inevitable happened. He was right – at 1 a.m. Jane Taylor died.

'Edward, can you do nothing yourself?' Mary Jane asked her husband.

He replied, bluntly, 'No! What can I do for a dead woman? Can I recall life?'

Dr Paterson was not finished with the Pritchard household yet. About one week after Mrs Taylor's death, he met Pritchard in the street who said he was going to Edinburgh the following day to bury his mother-in-law. Pritchard then asked Dr Paterson if, in his absence, he would be good enough to attend to his wife who was still suffering from gastric fever. Dr Paterson, knowing full well that she was not suffering from gastric fever, agreed. His subsequent examination only confirmed his initial suspicion of antimony poisoning. But, again, he said nothing.

In court, he explained himself by saying, 'I had no right. I was under no obligation.' Even after his second visit, he declined to share his suspicions of murder with anyone, not even with the patient herself. Nor did he return to see her after that because, he said, he did not actually consider her his patient. He did not see her again until the night she died. 'I had no right or title to go back and visit her,' he said. 'I would have considered myself intruding on the family had I done so.'

In court, he also said it might not have been safe to mention his suspicions to Dr Pritchard but he refused to expand on his comment, despite being asked by the Solicitor General to do so. Amazingly, he was allowed to remain silent on why he did not mention anything to the apparently worried husband. He did tell the court that he believed the same person who had poisoned Mrs Taylor was also poisoning Mrs Pritchard but he was not pressed to any great extent as to why he kept his own counsel and allowed the second woman to die.

He did, however, refuse to certify Mrs Taylor's cause of death. He returned the form to the Registrar of Deaths for Blythswood District with a note saying:

Dear Sir,

I am surprised that I am called on to certify the cause of death in this case. I only saw the person for a few minutes a very short period before her death. She seemed to be under some narcotic; but Dr Pritchard, who was present from the first moment of the illness until death occurred, and which happened in his own house, may certify the cause. The death was certainly sudden, unexpected and to me mysterious.

Pritchard duly obliged. According to him the cause of death was first paralysis and then apoplexy. At the time, no one seemed to notice that it should have been the other way round.

It was up to the letters pages of the press to criticise Dr Paterson's role in the affair. He and his Glasgow colleagues defended his position. But that came later – and too late to save Mrs Pritchard.

With Mrs Taylor out of the way, Dr Pritchard was free to make sure his wife was well looked after. He made her camomile tea and he gave it to Mary McLeod to serve to her. His wife vomited. On one occasion, he had Mary Patterson prepare an egg flip but he fetched the lump sugar himself to put in it. Curiously, the sugar came not from the kitchen, or even the dining room, but from his surgery. Mary Patterson sipped the drink before it was taken upstairs and announced, 'What a taste it has!' After drinking a glassful, Mrs Pritchard was violently ill – and so was Mary Patterson. The cook also fell victim to a piece of cheese she was asked to taste by the weakened Mary Jane – cheese provided by her husband. She felt a burning sensation in her throat, like pepper, and vomited throughout the night.

What is puzzling, throughout all this, is that no one, apart from Dr Paterson and he was keeping his lip tightly buttoned, seemed to smell a rat – the rat in question being the good Dr Pritchard who was about to deliver the coup de grâce on his hapless wife.

Although Mary Jane had being growing steadily weaker for months, she finally lost all sense of reality. Mary McLeod found her standing at the top of the stairs dressed only in her nightclothes and pointing at the floor saying, 'There is my poor mother dead again.' The maidservant called Mary Patterson and together they eased Mrs Pritchard back into bed. She complained of cramps in her hands and the servants began to rub them but the sick woman told them to leave her and rub her mother instead. Dr Paterson was called later that evening and was, it seems, greatly shocked by the change in the woman. If he had done something about it earlier, then perhaps that poor man's shock could have been avoided. There was, however, nothing he could do for her now. His silence had sentenced her to death.

At 1 a.m. on 18 March 1865, Mary McLeod was sent by Dr Pritchard to fetch a mustard poultice for his wife. By the time she returned, the poor woman's suffering was over – and Pritchard had launched into his greatest display yet of hypocrisy. He threw himself on the bed, begging her to come back to him. The two Marys watched the show – one of them no doubt remembering his promise to marry her should his wife die. Once he had regained his composure, Pritchard went downstairs to write some letters – to his own mother, to Mary Jane's relatives and to his bank, which was pressing him regarding an overdraft, and then he went out to post them. On his return, he told the cook a very strange story. 'Mary Jane walked down the street with me,' he said, 'and told me to take care of the girls but said nothing about the boys.' Then, he said, she kissed him and went away.

Again, he certified the death himself, in this case claiming it was gastric fever. She was to be buried beside her mother in Edinburgh's Grange Cemetery and, on Monday 20 March, he accompanied the body by train. The funeral was to take place on Thursday 23 March and, before interment, the body lay in the house of her father. Here, Pritchard treated spectators to another bizarre display of emotion. He asked for the lid to be removed and, as the family watched, he bent and kissed the cold, dead lips of his cold, dead wife.

'Those lips,' his defence counsel would later say, 'which his hand had closed, suppose that is the case. One would almost believe the thunderbolt of the Almighty would have stricken down the man who would have done it.' But obviously the Almighty was engaged elsewhere for there was no thunderbolt. However, there was one waiting for him back in Glasgow. Pritchard prepared to return home, no doubt believing that he had committed not one but two perfect murders. As far as he knew, no one suspected a thing. He was free and clear. But a conscience is a powerful thing – and someone's had finally been pricked.

The letter was anonymous but obviously written by an educated person. It arrived on the desk of Lanarkshire procurator fiscal William Hart shortly after Mrs Pritchard died. It read:

Sir,
Dr Pritchard's mother-in-law died suddenly and unexpectedly about three weeks ago in his house in Sauchiehall Street, Glasgow, under circumstances at least very suspicious. His wife died today, also suddenly and unexpectedly and under circumstances equally suspicious. We think it right to draw your attention to the above, as the proper person to take action in the matter and see justice done.

The letter was signed 'AMOR JUSTICIAE'.

Although never proved, the received wisdom is that the tip-off letter was the work of none other than Dr James Paterson. He confirmed he had discussed the matter with medical colleagues but denied he sent the letter, either personally or as part of a team. Even if he did have a hand in tipping off the authorities, the fact remains that what he did was too little, too late. Had he taken action after the death of Mrs Taylor, then perhaps Mary Jane Pritchard could have lived a long life.

As he sat in his first-class railway carriage, speeding home to Glasgow, Dr Pritchard had no idea that his plans had careered off track. He chatted to a fellow passenger, even giving him one of his trademark photographic calling cards, before getting off the train at Queen Street Railway Station. Perhaps there was a spring in his step – maybe even a smile on his lips and a song in his heart as he walked down the platform. But that spring became unsprung, the smile died and the song went badly out of tune when he was stopped by Superintendent McCall, of Glasgow City Police, who informed him that there was a warrant in existence for his arrest on the charge of murder. The bearded doctor had expected to be safely home in Clarence Place that night but, instead, he found himself occupying a cell in the city's North Prison on Duke Street. Later, he was transferred to Edinburgh's Calton Jail to await trial.

Naturally, he denied everything. He did not administer antimony to his dead wife – it was as simple as that. At this time, no one in his or his wife's families or even members of the public at large, for that matter, believed he was guilty. That changed when the post-mortem, carried out by Professor Douglas McLagan (who had examined the organs taken from Agnes Montgomery's body), Dr Arthur Gamgee and Dr Henry Littlejohn, showed that there were particles of antimony in the liver. However, despite their findings, Pritchard's protestations of innocence did not alter one jot. And when Mrs Taylor's body was exhumed, examined and found to contain antimony, he never wavered. He was innocent.

Even when evidence that he had bought the poison came to light, it failed to dent his apparent confidence.

He impressed many people by his calm and gentle disposition. He prayed. He insisted he was unjustly accused. He prayed some more. His defence counsel expressed a feeling that not guilty and not proven verdicts were unlikely. But Pritchard said cheerily, 'Keep up your heart, we will return to Glasgow together.'

The trial, it seems, was the most eagerly awaited hearing since that of Madeleine Smith who was accused but acquitted of poisoning her lover in 1857. Pritchard's trial began in Edinburgh on Monday 3 July 1865 and would last five days. Newspaper reporters from all over the country descended on the capital and the courtroom had to be specially adapted to allow them to report the proceedings to their rapt readers. Meanwhile, those members of the public who wanted to hear it for themselves crowded into Parliament Square to await the opening of the doors. Some of the lucky few – generally those of higher birth – had special tickets which meant they did not need to mingle with the great unwashed and were allowed in first. However, as soon as the doors opened officially, there was a rush for the remaining spaces. The upper and lower public galleries were filled to capacity and every available bit of space – standing and sitting – was taken. This was the trial of the year and every member of the eager audience craned forward, anxious for their first glimpse of the killer doctor.

Pritchard had been brought from Calton Jail at eight that morning. A huge crowd had followed the prison wagon up the High Street and into Parliament Square. At three minutes past ten, he was brought into the courtroom to take his place in the dock. His brother Charles had been given special permission to sit with him and the customary two policemen. Dressed in black – he was, after all, still in mourning for his wife and mother-in-law – the accused took off his hat and gave the spectators a chance to size him up.

According to one description, he was tall, stout and well built – although his weeks in prison had seen him lose some weight. His hair was long but he was bald on top and he sported what is now known as a comb-over. But the most distinctive thing about him was his beard, of which he was inordinately proud. In fact, one of the only complaints he made while in prison was that he was not allowed pomatum, an apple-scented ointment, to treat his whiskers.

When the three judges took their seats on the bench, the accused rose and bowed solemnly. Then he sat back down and adopted his now customary melancholy but calm demeanour as he listened to the evidence against him. Only occasionally during the five-day trial did he show any form of emotion: when two of his children told the court how happy they were with mama and papa a handkerchief was pressed to his eyes; when mention was made of his wife, he showed sadness; and, finally, when Mary McLeod gave her evidence. Then, according to one observer, a change came over him and the calm appearance was replaced by a distinctly malignant look. For Mary McLeod, albeit with some hesitation, was the one witness who changed everything for him. Once her testimony was over, Pritchard was revealed as a calculating adulterer who had, in all probability, turned killer.

In the summer of 1864, Mrs Pritchard had caught her husband kissing the then fifteen-year-old Mary in one of the bedrooms of the house. Afterwards, an affronted Mary spoke to Mrs Pritchard and offered to leave but the woman would not hear of it. She told Mary she would speak to her husband who, she said, was a 'nasty dirty man'. However, the affair did not stop there. Under pressure in the witness box, Mary admitted that the accused 'had connection', a euphemism for sexual intercourse, with her and she 'became with child to him'. On being told of this, he said he would put it right and gave her some medicine. Soon after, she suffered a miscarriage.

And still their affair continued. Their 'connection' carried on. He gave her presents – namely, a ring, a brooch and a locket. His fondness for handing out photographs of himself saw him giving her his likeness to put in the locket. Mary was wearing the locket in court but there was no photograph inside because, she said, she had torn it up. He had even promised the girl marriage. On being questioned in court regarding this, Mary became somewhat incoherent, being unwilling to say exactly what Pritchard promised her. Under pressure from the prosecution and the Court – even to the extent of threatening her with prison – she admitted, 'He said that when Mrs Pritchard died, if she died before him, and I was alive, he would marry me.'

Mary had been arrested at around the same time as Pritchard but, after two days in custody, she was released without charge. The defence tried to suggest that it was the girl who committed the murders in order to have Pritchard all to herself but it was a half-hearted attempt and never really held much water. It was, as the prosecution insisted, murder with a doctor's finger in it.

It is not necessary for the prosecution to provide a motive for murder but it always helps. His affair with young Mary was one possible motive. Either he wanted his wife out of the way so that they could be together (possible but unlikely) or Mary Jane had threatened to expose him for the dirty old man he was (equally as possible but equally as unlikely). Then there was his financial state to consider. He was considerably overdrawn at the bank and he would have stood to inherit some cash but not enough to merit the extreme action he had taken. Similarly, no real motive was established for the murder of his mother-in-law. Perhaps she suspected he was systematically poisoning her daughter and so had to be silenced. Perhaps she just got in the way of his plan. She had also caught him dallying with young Mary and perhaps that contributed to his desire to kill her.

In the end, the jury took only fifty-five minutes to find him guilty of both charges. On passing sentence, the Lord Justice Clerk, Lord Inglis, said, 'The evidence leaves in the mind of no reasonable man the slightest doubt of your guilt.' He put the black cap on and pronounced sentence of death. Pritchard was

to be taken back to Glasgow under escort, to be fed bread and water until 28th July and, on that day, between the hours eight and ten forenoon, to be taken furth the said prison to the common place of execution of the burgh of Glasgow, or to such place as the Magistrates of Glasgow shall appoint as the place of execution, and there, at the hands of the common executioner, be hanged by the neck until dead; and ordain his body thereafter to be buried within the precincts of the said prison of Glasgow, further ordain his whole moveable goods and gear to be escheat and forfeit to the Crown.

As he removed the black cap, he added, 'Which is pronounced for doom. May God Almighty have mercy upon your soul.'

Dr Pritchard bowed deeply, first to the jury and then to bench and, leaning heavily on the arm of the police officer to his right, was helped down from the courtroom to the cells.

The verdict was met with no uproar. Even in 1865, there were those who deplored the idea of capital punishment and appealed for mercy for the cruellest of murderers. But, for Pritchard, there was no such plea. As they had for John Thomson, the kind-hearted abolitionists kept their silence.

For his part, the condemned man contented himself with reading the Bible and ingratiating himself with his jailers – and in implicating his former lover in his crimes. He admitted he had killed his dear wife but that young Mary had been involved by knowingly serving her the poisoned food. This was greeted with universal disbelief. One Episcopalian minister told him he did not believe a word he had said and that his crimes were almost unexampled. Pritchard was sitting on his bed. He threw himself back, stretching out his hands, and said, 'Do you know, Doctor MacLeod, I now understand how Jesus suffered from the unbelief of men in His Word.'

In a second confession, he claimed he had killed Mary Jane with chloroform, again insisting Mary McLeod had been involved. But of the murder of his mother-in-law he was innocent. Still this was not accepted. Finally, he admitted both murders and fully cleared Mary McLeod of any involvement. He had committed the crimes while under 'a species of terrible madness and the use of ardent spirits,' he said.

His last letter was to his wife's brother, Dr Michael Taylor. It began:

> Farewell, brother, I die 20 hours from now. Romans viii, 34 to 39 verses. Mary Jane, Darling Mother, and you, I will meet, as you said the last time you spoke to me, in happier circumstances. Bless you and yours, prays the dying penitent.

Rain fell during the night of Thursday–Friday 27–28 July and the morning was dampened by constant drizzle. The scaffold, as was the custom, had been erected on Glasgow Green, opposite the High Court and the South Prison. The city's main Fair was underway and the Green was filled with stalls and booths, which had to be removed in order for the public hanging to take place. Perhaps the Fair was the reason so many people turned up to witness Pritchard's end. Some estimates state there were upwards of 100,000 thronging the Green, with 750 police officers – most of the city's force – keeping order and pushing the crowds behind specially constructed barriers.

The object of their interest had been brought from the North Prison the previous evening and lodged in its southern counterpart. As he sat in the condemned cell awaiting his final hour, the streets around Jail Square were filled with people picking their vantage spot to view the morning's entertainment. The day dawned damp and grey and the streets began to clog. Preachers, never the men to miss the opportunity of a crowd to harangue, drifted among the people distributing religious tracts with words of warning against the descent into sin. By six in the morning the crowd had grown considerably and clouds of pungent smoke rose towards the looming skies as innumerable pipes were fired up. It was a fitting send-off for a man who once wrote a paper on the uses and misuses of tobacco. Faces pressed against every window in every building with a view of the square while lines of people could even be seen across the river.

At 7.15 a.m., a ripple of excitement washed through the masses as hangman William Calcraft climbed the steps of the scaffold to make his pre-execution checks. Then, at eight, the star attraction made his appearance, his head held high, still dressed in mourning but fashionably so. He walked steadily towards his death – 'as if marching to music' said one observer. As the crowd shouted insults – not just at him but also at the hangman for, despite the enjoyment many had from a 'topping', his duties were never popular. From the platform, Pritchard announced, 'I acknowledge the justice of my sentence.' He did not waver as the hood was pulled over his head and Calcraft draped the noose around his neck, experiencing a little trouble with Pritchard's long hair and bushy beard. Although he retained his composure throughout, a slight swaying from side to side did betray his anxiety. The bolt was drawn and his body made the last drop. A low moan seeped from the crowd and one reporter described how 'he shrugged his shoulder more than half-a-dozen times, his head shook and the whole body trembled'. Calcraft reached out to the rope to steady the swinging body then let it go. The body twisted in the noose a few times and the kid gloves Pritchard had been holding slipped from his fingers. After a minute, the convulsions eased until there was only some twitching in the hands. And, two minutes later, Dr Pritchard was still. His was the last public execution in Glasgow.

An open coffin yawned beneath the drop and, after the body had hung for a time, it was simply allowed to fall into it. It landed with such force that it damaged the wood and a team of joiners had to rush forward to repair the break. His body was buried in the graveyard of the South Prison, a stone with the letter P rudely scratched on it marking the spot. But his body would not be permitted to rest in peace. In 1910, when the court buildings were being renovated, the body was exhumed. The coffin shattered under the blows of workmen's shovels but the remains inside were found to be remarkably intact. The clothes, including a pair of elastic-sided boots, that he wore on the scaffold were still in relatively good condition. Both the boots and the skull were purloined by an enterprising workman and later sold.

Someone, then, was literally walking around in dead man's shoes.

5

FRENCH KISSES

Eugène Marie Chantrelle

There was nothing like a sensational murder trial to get Victorian Britain buzzing. Of course, the principal players in the mortal tragedy had to come from the proper classes. Violent death was not uncommon among the denizens of the slum-lands and thieves' kitchens that clogged the nation's cities and so was not of interest to polite society. The poor and the starving and those of loose morals were, for the most part, better out of sight and out of mind. But a trial involving the middle or upper classes was different – and, in the early summer of 1878, Edinburgh was agog with a case that brimmed with sensation. There was a handsome Frenchman, a beautiful young girl, seduction, sexual adventure, jealousy, violence and, finally, murder. Hell, this case had it all.

Although his Edinburgh employers at Newington Academy were not aware of it at first, Frenchman Eugène Marie Chantrelle had a chequered past. As time went on, they looked at him differently but, at first, he seemed to be just what they were looking for to tutor their young ladies. In December 1865, he presented credentials that seemed to prove he had gained a Bachelor of Arts degree in Paris although it is now doubtful he ever graduated. He told the Academy's proprietor James McLachlan that he had come direct from Paris to Edinburgh to study medicine but had dropped out after a year. In actual fact, the then thirty-one-year-old Chantrelle had studied for five years in Strasbourg and Paris, as well as the single year in Edinburgh. He had been born in Nantes and had taken a medical course there but, by 1851, he was in Paris manning the student barricades during the communistic rebellion of that year. During one skirmish, a sabre-wielding soldier wounded the young Chantrelle. At the end of hostilities, he found himself on the losing side and realised that life in France was too hot for him so he took himself off to America. His movements there are shrouded in mystery but, by 1862, he was in England teaching French at several schools.

What Chantrelle would not have told his potential employer in Edinburgh was that he was a man of enormous sexual appetites – and that they had already earned him a nine-month spell in prison for sexually assaulting one of his pupils in England. Naturally, had Mr McLachlan known this, he would never have offered the man the position at his school. But he did not know and so Chantrelle took his place among the staff of the Arniston Place school, teaching the proper young ladies French and Latin. And it was in the classroom that his eye fell on fourteen-year-old Elizabeth Cullen Dyer.

Mr McLachlan described her as 'short in stature, good looking, prepossessing in manner and well liked'. He also said she was of a lively and cheerful disposition, kindly and malleable except when she was thwarted – if she were put down in her class she would show how she felt. She was also high spirited but of quick temper. Chantrelle, being Chantrelle, would have been aware of her immediately and she, it seems, was also well aware of him. He was, despite being more than twice her age, an attractive man – tall, well built, well dressed and magnificently whiskered in the style of the day. Add to that the fact that he had an accent that could melt a lady's heart in just a few syllables and it is little wonder a young girl would fall for him.

He insisted he had known her for eighteen months before anything romantic took place between them. According to him, they met by chance at a lecture out of school while she was in the company of her brother John. As they walked home afterwards, John disappeared with another young lady, leaving Elizabeth alone with the older teacher. It proved the beginning of their courtship – although the ever-gallant Monsieur insisted that nothing could take place between them until he had first met with her parents. At least that was what he said later. At Elizabeth's suggestion, he duly turned up at the Dyer house only to find that the young girl had not first asked her father's permission.

Whatever the truth of the matter, the affair was swiftly common knowledge among the girls of the Academy and it was finally brought to Mr McLachlan's attention by a school superintendent who said that M. Chantrelle was 'paying particular attention to Miss Dyer' and giving her presents of jewellery. According to the superintendent, 'it was notorious among the other pupils'.

Elizabeth's mother had complained previously that her daughter was not coming home from school at the proper hour so, after some inquiry, Mr McLachlan informed her that Elizabeth was going to the house of M. Chantrelle for extra lessons. On being challenged, Elizabeth refused to end the inappropriate liaison. The situation was a bit of a mess – and it was about to get worse. At some stage, the private tutoring changed from the romance languages to the language of romance. It soon became obvious that there were more than just verbs being conjugated, for at the age of sixteen, Elizabeth Dyer fell pregnant. Chantrelle, however, expressed some doubt over paternity. In a letter, she assures him, 'I tell you I never gave myself to anyone but you.' In another, she pleads, 'If it was broken off I would die. You think perhaps that I do not mean it but really I could not live without your love.'

Her family was, quite naturally, outraged. There was some friction between Chantrelle and her father – so much so that Elizabeth wrote, 'Will you settle it with Papa and tell him to say yes or no? If no, then we must be married without his consent as I could not live without you . . .' At one point, in October 1867, she released him from all his promises and was expressing a desire to die but, by the following April, after her pregnancy was discovered, she was back in the full flush of romantic love, writing, 'All I want on earth is to be always with you. I would be as happy as the day is long, which I am not now . . . I tell you again, Eugène, that no one ever had me, never . . .'

Chantrelle was, according to his own letters, 'ready to fulfil all my engagements with you when the time comes, even though it should bring me shame and misery.' So, in August 1868, the couple were married in her father's house in Buccleuch Place. She was already seven months pregnant by this time and she gave birth to their first son in October. Chantrelle, citing his medical training, delivered the child himself in their home at 81a George Street. They eventually had four children together although one did not survive.

They remained married for over nine years but it was not a happy match. Despite having done the decent thing and married the girl, no doubt against all his natural instincts to flee the city, Chantrelle proved to be a far from ideal husband. He had lost his position at Newington Academy through the scandal and often found himself in straitened financial conditions. But he never lost his taste for wine, women and song. He was a regular customer at various brothels in Castle Street and St James Square. There, his sexual appetites, violent nature and pretensions to medical qualifications earned him a number of nicknames – including 'The Bawdy Doctor' and 'The Black Doctor'. According to one brothel keeper, he was considered 'a very dirty man by the girls' and 'a horrible man in his practices'.

Barbara Kay, who kept Polly Scott's house in Castle Street, said he was a customer for years, sometimes attending three or four times a week. One girl, Annie Clark, said he 'had been very beastly' and had taken unnatural liberties with her but had not 'had connection' with her, which meant there was no actual intercourse. What those 'unnatural liberties' were can only be guessed at – although another girl said he was 'a very coarse man' who used to carry surgical instruments around with him and he wanted to use them on the girls. It was stated that he would have several girls in the room with him at one time, all naked, and he would select one or two to go to bed with him. He generally supplied champagne and paid around ten shillings for their favours – a tidy sum in those days.

He also had a temper and, when he was drunk, it often manifested itself violently. With a loaded pistol in his hand, he once kept a girl in his room overnight, swearing he would blow her brains out if anyone tried to enter. On another occasion, he chased a girl through the house armed with the same pistol.

The girls said he never seemed short of money. He earned some cash by providing private French tutoring and also by giving unofficial medical treatment – generally to acquaintances and to fellow French émigrés. One, a woman, admitted receiving some sort of treatment from him but refused to divulge the nature of the illness, which suggested it may have been a sexually transmitted disease or perhaps an abortion.

As his conviction in England proved, he was not above forcing himself on a woman. In January 1867, a Miss Ellen Lucy Holme applied for the position of housekeeper in the Chantrelle home. She was shown into the dining room to be interviewed by Chantrelle who listened sympathetically as she relayed to him how unhappy she was, living with her father, a clergyman, and her stepmother, who was 'not kind'. Miss Holme, then around twenty-seven, was grateful for his kind words but then things turned nasty. He attacked her, threw her down on the floor and, one hand clamped over her mouth to stifle her screams, raped her. This one act of 'forcible connection' made her pregnant and she gave birth to his illegitimate son in September that year. She was adamant that Chantrelle, and only Chantrelle, could possibly be the father.

That he owned a pistol was common knowledge – especially after an incident during a holiday in Portobello when one of his sons got hold of it and fired it, slightly injuring both his brother and his father. Elizabeth was also no stranger to her husband's rages – or, indeed, the pistol. He often threatened her with it and even blasted away at a door in the house to practise his aim. Not content with taking out his abusive rages on the working girls, he also regularly turned on his wife. On one occasion, again while on holiday in Portobello, he stayed out all night and when he returned, Elizabeth had gone to bed. In a subsequent letter, she told her mother:

> I might have been sleeping for about an hour or more when I was awakened by several blows. I got one on the side of the head which knocked me stupid. When I came to myself I could not move my face and this morning I find my jaw bone out of its place, my mouth inside skinned and festering and my face all swollen. The servants who sleep in the next room heard it all . . . they heard him say that he would make mincemeat out of me. And terrible language . . .'

She told her mother that he had often threatened to kill her. He said he would use his medical knowledge to poison her in such a way that no one would ever detect it. Elizabeth was desperately unhappy and the love she had felt – or at least thought she had felt – quickly died in the early days of the marriage. She told one servant, Jemima McGregor, that she hated her husband, that she had married too young and had known no better. According to Jemima, Elizabeth said she'd had another sweetheart before Chantrelle, a draper, who she had liked better. Divorce, though, was not an option. There had already been enough scandal attached to the family thanks to the manner of the marriage.

She also knew of her husband's sexual proclivities, telling the servant that she was convinced he was visiting 'a bad house'. She said her husband had told her that, in France, this was common – a husband would go with other women with his wife's knowledge while a wife would go with other men.

Jemima witnessed Chantrelle's abuse. She often heard the couple arguing and, on one occasion, the master threatened to pull up his wife's clothes and 'whip her bottom'. He actually pulled her over his knee and started to hitch up her skirts. Jemima, for decency's sake, looked away, but she heard him beating Elizabeth. She said he often called his wife a whore and a bitch. 'I think Mr Chantrelle was not a proper person,' she said.

Sometimes the abuse would be too much for Elizabeth and she would go home to her mother – despite the fact that some of her family had no sympathy for her because of the circumstances surrounding her wedding. But, each time, she would return to Chantrelle – and more violence. Given that she was so miserable, it will come as no surprise that she sought solace in other men. Jemima McGregor said that Madame Chantrelle received visits from a Mr Gillespie, a clerk who worked in rooms below their apartment. The servant said that she often heard them together, alone in a room. Later Mme Chantrelle confessed that Mr Gillespie had kissed her but, as Jemima said, 'from her hair being down and the state of her dress I thought they had been doing more than kissing'.

Chantrelle heard about the affair after his wife sacked Jemima McGregor. The twenty-four-year-old maid was a good-looking young woman and it seems Mme Chantrelle was convinced she and her husband had been enjoying a dalliance. Jemima did not take the termination of employment, or the accusation of adultery, lying down for, one night, she and her aunt returned to the Chantrelle house to have it out with Elizabeth. During the resulting argument, she accused Elizabeth of taking men into the house while her husband was out. Mr Gillespie downstairs was named and he eventually gave Chantrelle a written apology for behaving in such an inappropriate manner. A young man, who worked at the bank, was also named and, at first, Mme Chantrelle denied this but, after some pressing – no doubt violently – she admitted to 'repeated adulterous intercourse' with him. Chantrelle challenged the man and, through blackmail, wrung a £50 solatium out of him in return for not informing his employers about his improprieties. Chantrelle later said this money was donated to a hospital in his hometown of Nantes but, given his expensive tastes in nightlife and his meagre bank balance, this was probably not the case.

Chantrelle magnanimously forgave Elizabeth for her indiscretions.

However, according to Chantrelle, life with his beloved was no bed of roses. Although he admitted she was seldom ill and, when she was, she preferred him to treat her, he said, 'My wife did have her peculiarities. I do not know if she thought I was sufficiently attentive to her. I was as attentive to her as I could be. I had a great deal to do. I was not at all jealous of her.'

However robust her physical health, he claimed her mental state was far from stable. As well as flouncing out of the house without the slightest provocation, she also, more than once, threatened suicide. To an extent, this picture of a delicate mental condition is borne out by the tone of some of her earlier letters, in which she is given to dramatic flourishes of romantic language, but how much of what Chantrelle subsequently claimed is true can only be guessed. He said that she threatened to drown herself. On one occasion, he told her to 'go and do it' and she stormed from the house. Later, he went out on other business and subsequently met up with her. She said to him, 'You are a nice man to let me go and drown myself.'

He replied, 'You have been going to do that so often that I cannot always be running after you to prevent it.'

At other times, he would come into her bedroom, where she washed herself in a tub, to find her ready to put her face in the water. Sometimes she would appear to be in a swoon and he would lay her on the bed and rub her hands to bring her round – despite the fact that he did not believe she had actually fainted while in the water. He told her that, one of these times, he would leave her all night in the bath. On one occasion, he found her on the floor apparently in a dead faint. He told her she had not convinced him and she did not try that trick again. He said she was in the habit of reading 'penny trashy novels' and this was her attempt at recreating scenes from them.

He appeared indignant when she accused him of paying attention to other women, which was a bit of a cheek considering his nocturnal activities. She objected to him tipping his hat to female students but, bearing in mind how she got involved with him, it was perhaps not unreasonable that she requested him not to do this. He also claimed she once accused him of watching a woman in a lodging house across the street and 'stroking his chin at her'. He lost a family of lodgers because she believed he was having an affair with the mother. She firmly believed he was playing around with Jemima McGregor although her suspicions in this case might well have been groundless.

But one thing she did know for certain was that he had insured her life for £1,000. 'Mama,' she said to her mother on one occasion, 'my life is insured now and you will see that my life will go soon.'

Things in the Chantrelle household were deteriorating badly. With Chantrelle's volatile nature, his extra-marital activities, his wife's suspicions and a meagre bank balance, something was bound to happen.

In the early hours of Wednesday 2 January 1878, the Chantrelles' new servant, Mary Byrne, heard a strange moaning coming from her mistress's bedchamber. She knew that she and the master had not slept together for some time and Mme Chantrelle had retired early the previous night complaining of feeling unwell. She had already vomited once and had been suffering from a severe headache. As was her custom, she took their youngest child, then aged thirteen months, to bed with her. Chantrelle said that he had heard the child crying through the night and had taken the baby from his wife's bed in order that she was not disturbed.

Mary Byrne, hearing the odd sounds, went into Mme Chantrelle's room and found her unconscious. She called M. Chantrelle and he came in, obviously having been roused from bed. He looked at his wife and then told Mary he could hear the baby crying. She went to see to the child who was still fast asleep. When she returned to Mme Chantrelle's room, she saw the master walking back from the window and could smell a strong odour of gas.

Dr James Carmichael had a practice in Burntisland but lived in

Edinburgh's Northumberland Street. Although he was known to Chantrelle, for both were members of the Red Cross Knight Order of Masons, he was surprised to find the man at his front door, asking him to come to his house for his wife was very ill. He knew Chantrelle lived in George Street and other doctors lived close by but there he was at his door. Dr Carmichael accompanied the tall Frenchman back to his home. There, he found the patient lying 'profoundly unconscious' in bed in a back room. She was obviously very ill as she looked extremely pale. Dr Carmichael said with 'her respiration very much interrupted', she was 'breathing at intervals only'. He could smell gas and he ordered that the woman be moved into a front room. Chantrelle said that he did not know where the gas was coming from – he had checked the pipes and turned off the stopcock. The doctor suggested that the supply should be turned off at the meter and Mary Byrne was sent to do so.

Had he not smelled the gas, the doctor might have thought at first Mme Chantrelle had been poisoned or drugged. Her eyes were virtually insensible to light – there was a slight contraction when the flame of a candle was brought closer but, in the main, the pupils were immobile. Although this could be one symptom of poisoning, there was no sign of the muscle contractions, spasms or sweating which he might also expect to see. There was some evidence of cyanosis – blueness – around the lips and traces of vomit on the bed sheets and pillowcase. When he arrived, he also spotted some matter oozing from the side of her mouth and he dislodged a wedge of what appeared to be orange pulp from her mouth.

However, the plain and simple truth of it was that Dr Carmichael could smell gas. So he sent a note to Dr Henry Littlejohn, a professional toxicologist, who was also the police surgeon for the City of Edinburgh, saying, 'If you wish to see a case of coal-gas poisoning, I should like you to come up here at once.'

Dr Carmichael had suggested that a nip of brandy should be given to the unconscious woman but, as he waited for Dr Littlejohn, he noted that the level of spirits in the bottle was falling steadily and neither he nor the patient was drinking it. Clearly, M. Chantrelle had been imbibing heavily throughout the morning but that could easily be put down to worry over his wife's health. Artificial respiration was attempted but nothing could revive the woman. When Dr Littlejohn arrived he thought she was dead and ordered that she be removed to the city's Royal Infirmary.

Being a police surgeon, he knew something of the troubles between the Chantrelles for, on at least two occasions, his law-enforcement colleagues had been called to the house. He went into the back room with Dr Carmichael to trace the source of the gas leak but could find nothing. The apparently worried husband had been told to remain with his wife and continue the artificial respiration but, much to the surprise of the medical men, he gave up and joined them in the back room. Again he said he could not account for the smell of gas, suggesting that it was perhaps coming up through the floorboards.

Elizabeth Chantrelle was taken to the Royal Infirmary where she died at four o'clock that afternoon. Dr Littlejohn and Dr Douglas MacLagan, who had worked together in the Pritchard case, conducted the post-mortem. By the end of it, they were unsure what exactly had killed the young woman but they were certain of one thing – it was not gas. They noted no bright patches on the skin as they would expect to find and there was no odour when they opened the cavities, in particular the lungs. The woman's blood was dark and fluid – in cases of coal-gas poisoning, the blood was usually more florid in colour. They would also have expected to find a smell of gas from the brain but, when the skull was opened, there was no such odour.

They had no doubt the woman had been poisoned. They just didn't know with what.

Elizabeth Cullen Dyer Chantrelle was buried in her wedding dress on 5 January in Edinburgh's Grange Cemetery – the same burial place of both Mrs Pritchard and her mother. Eugène was the very image of the grieving husband, even attempting to throw himself into the open grave after his beloved. It was a fine display of emotion and by all accounts an impressive performance. Yet a performance was all it was. Eugène Marie Chantrelle was no devoted husband, left desolate by the sudden death of his young wife. He was a lying, cheating, scheming, whore-monger who had systematically abused his wife for years before callously murdering her in order to obtain the £1,000 from the insurance policy he had taken out on her life. He had boasted he would poison her in such a way that no one would ever detect it. With the finest medical brains in Edinburgh scratching their heads over the cause of death, he probably thought he would be laughing all the way to the bank.

But those fine medical brains were still convinced the woman had been poisoned. Their initial examination of the body revealed little. However, their study of the vomit on the bed sheets proved very enlightening. They found traces of grapes and orange in the sample while her stomach contents revealed she had eaten both fruits. But it wasn't the fruit that was to be her husband's undoing. Chemical analysis revealed traces of opium – and a police investigation discovered that M. Chantrelle had bought a large supply of that very drug. But, although they found a selection of narcotics and poisons in Chantrelle's study – used in his unofficial medical duties – they found no opium.

And examination of the gas supply revealed that a pipe under the window – the one Mary Byrne had seen Chantrelle walking away from – had been sabotaged. Quite obviously, someone had simply twisted the thin pipe until it ruptured.

On his return from the funeral, Chantrelle was arrested. He denied everything, of course, suggesting his wife was capable of taking her own life, that she suffered from depression, that she had threatened to kill herself with laudanum, which was an opium-based sedative.

It has to be said that the case against him was largely circumstantial. Apart from the fact he had bought a supply of opium, there was no evidence that he had actually administered it to her, either in the fruit or in lemonade he was known to have bought and served at New Year. Even when the body was exhumed for further examination, scientists could still find no trace of the poison. But the abuse he inflicted on her during their nine years together, coupled with his sexual adventures among the city's working girls and the existence of the recently purchased insurance policy, all combined to convince the Crown they had a case for murder and Chantrelle was remanded in custody.

The French Consul in Edinburgh took an interest in the case and requested that the Crown Office supply a copy of the indictment. In a letter, the consul said that as this 'was the first time in living memory that a Frenchman of some notoriety is tried for murder in Scotland, the Law Office (of the Foreign Office in Paris) feel a very natural curiosity to know intimately the proceedings of your Court of Justice in such a case.' The indictment also caused a very public falling-out between the proprietors and editor of the *Edinburgh Evening News* and the procurator fiscal's office. The newspaper published an extract from the indictment prior to it being made public. The Crown Office and procurator fiscal wanted to know how such a leak happened, insisting that no such indictment had been in existence when the newspaper printed its story on 8 April 1878. The newspaper revealed that the information came from someone they considered reliable and added that they 'had no expectation that its publication should have caused surprise to any one, seeing that the case is one in which considerable public interest taken'. They also chided the authorities, saying:

> If gentlemen occupying official positions would deal more generously with the press and give access to documents of public interest as soon as they could do so, consistently with the proper discharge of their duties, complaints of this kind could be less numerous. It is impossible even in the High Court of Justiciary for our reporters to obtain an indictment until a prisoner pleads, while according to your letter it is public property as soon as it is served.

While Chantrelle sat in Edinburgh's Calton Jail preparing his defence – asking for various scientific books from his home to assist him – the authorities continued to build their case. The procurator fiscal travelled north to Inverness to interview Jemima McGregor whom, he knew, had been with the accused 'when a matter of some delicacy' was discussed – namely, his wife's infidelities. The procurator fiscal also applied for permission from the Crown Office to pay Mary Byrne the sum of seven shillings per week for room and board until the trial. After the murder, she had taken up service in a house in Murrayfield but had resigned when her new employers refused to let her attend chapel. She was staying with friends but planned to go back to Ireland if she could not find another job. The Crown Office said that payment 'would be expedient in this case'.

The sensational nature of the trial prompted some of the good and solid citizens, who had things to add to the Crown case, to request they be excused from giving evidence. Doctors' notes were produced and excuses were given as they tried to distance themselves from the racy events.

Meanwhile, in a note, the procurator fiscal said that the witnesses were more or less respectable, 'except numbers 67 to 71 who are connected to houses of ill fame'. One of these witnesses was out of town, obviously on the run with her husband for whom there was a warrant on a charge of assault. She said she would return if her expenses were met. With these delicate matters in mind, the procurator fiscal thought it might be advisable to accommodate the witnesses of higher rank separately from the domestic servants, tradesmen and those connected with houses of ill fame.

While some witnesses were doing what they could to get out of being associated with the case, the public at large was fascinated with the scandal. As was now the custom in such high profile trials, tickets were issued for those with influence to get into the courtroom without having to crowd with the lower ranks and a special notice was posted regarding the conduct of the trial to begin on Tuesday 7 May 1878. One of the strictures was that 'no money be taken at the doors for admission to any part of the court'. There had been occasions in the past, including the 1844 trial of Christina Gilmour for poisoning her husband, when doorkeepers had allegedly taken cash for access to the public galleries.

Chantrelle had his lawyers contact the procurator fiscal regarding items of clothing he wanted to wear in prison and at the trial. They were a fancy black cloth frock coat, dark tweed trousers and braces, six collars, six pairs of cuffs, six pocket handkerchiefs, hat, black gloves, sprung boots (new), hairbrush, comb, clothes brush. Clearly, he intended looking his best for his public performance.

Chantrelle's defence team could do little to counteract the evidence against their client. They tried to show that the medical evidence was largely inconclusive, that no poison was found in the body, that the symptoms displayed by the deceased prior to death did not fully fit that of opium poisoning but that was all they could do. And, at the end of their cross examination, a rather petulant Chantrelle demanded, 'Is that *all* the evidence for the defence?'

Despite this, Chantrelle was still convinced he would be acquitted and had even arranged for a cab to be waiting outside the courtroom to whisk him away as soon as he was free. However, at the end of the four-day trial, the jury took less than an hour to find him guilty. Chantrelle, surprised that his protestations of innocence had not been believed, asked to say a few words. He then proceeded to claim that someone else had rubbed the opium into the vomit. He began to ramble and grow excited, forcing the Lord Justice Clerk to cut him short, telling him, if he had anything further to say, to do so through his lawyer.

As he sat in the condemned cell at Calton Jail, Chantrelle seemed to resign himself to his fate. However, he did not, like many others, take refuge in religion even though he was certain he would be 'sharing a pipe with the Devil'. On his last night, instead of indulging in prayer, he replied, when asked if he had any last requests, 'Three bottles of champagne and sex.' Naturally, this was not supplied but he did enjoy a breakfast of coffee, eggs and bread and butter. He did take part in a religious service prior to his final walk but this was unlikely to have been motivated by any need for forgiveness. When asked if he had anything to get off his chest, he announced, 'I have no confession to make.'

At 7.30 a.m. on Friday 31 May 1878, the official witnesses gathered in the yard of Calton Jail for the hanging. It was an occasion for some degree of pomp. The magistrates were magnificently robed and carried long white poles. Police and prison officers were resplendent in dress uniforms and carried gleaming halberds (a combination of spear and battleaxe). The hangman was William Marwood, a cobbler from Lincolnshire, credited with devising the 'long drop', a method of hanging that broke the accused's neck rather than risk slow strangulation. Like Pritchard, Chantrelle was dressed in the mourning clothes he wore at his wife's funeral. He seemed cool and self-possessed as he mounted the scaffold but observers did note he looked haggard.

There was little sympathy for Chantrelle but the prison chaplain, during a short service in the warden's office, did ask God to 'give strength unto him in this terrible hour . . . and let not the terrors of death fall upon him'. The terrors of death did not fall on him but he was looking pale as he walked from the warden's office to the storeroom where the scaffold had been erected. There was a burly prison guard on either side of him and a procession of dignitaries and witnesses behind him. When he entered the room, he looked around at the cloth-covered boxes piled high all around and his nose twitched at the strong stench of oakum, a loose fibre twisted from old hemp ropes, the creation of which was a common form of employment for convicts. Then Chantrelle's eyes fell on the trapdoor and, for the first time, he hesitated, perhaps only then feeling the chill breeze of his own mortality. The witnesses filed away to their vantage points as the prison officers led the pinioned prisoner to his place over the drop. Although he had been refused his champagne earlier, he did receive a small glass of whisky prior to the bolt being pulled. After Chantrelle drank his whisky,

Marwood strapped his legs together with a leather belt, pulled a white cap over his head and then pulled the bolt.

Marwood's expertise was well employed that day for the Frenchman died without a struggle. Outside, a black flag was sent fluttering up the prison flagpole to inform the usual crowd on Calton Hill that the deed was done. The body hung under the level scaffold for about an hour before it was cut down and wrapped in cloth. He was buried, coated in quicklime, within the prison walls.

Such was the interest in the case and his final hours that the Glasgow *Evening Times* published a special edition to give their readers a detailed account of the event.

Chantrelle had the dubious honour of being the first person to be hanged in Calton Jail. He was not, however, the first person in Scotland to be executed in private instead of having to endure the public spectacle that the likes of Dr Pritchard went through. That particular honour went to tramp George Chalmers who was executed within the old County Prison at Perth in 1870 for the murder of toll-keeper John Miller in Braco.

6

SHADOW OF THE NOOSE

Peter Queen

The slender, sallow-faced man burst into the police office at 3 a.m. in the morning and made a quite astounding statement. 'Go to 539 Dumbarton Road,' he said. 'I think you will find my wife dead there.'

Even in the Glasgow of 1931 – razor-gang city where, if its reputation was to be believed, violence stalked the streets and death lurked at every corner – such claims were not made every night. But the police did not simply rush out into the November chill to see if there was indeed a body on the second floor of the specified tenement.

The man certainly seemed nervous and not a little excited – just as you would expect. But, when he was asked what happened, he failed to answer. So he was asked again and then a third time. Finally he responded – and the words he used became the central plank in the case against him. For, if the police version of the sentence is correct, then the man may well have murdered the woman he claimed was his wife. But, if the man's version was true, then he may well have been innocent of homicide.

The expert witnesses employed by the defence would further complicate the matter. They were at the very top of their profession but even they could not agree whether there had been a murder at all.

And in the centre of it all was a man standing in the shadow of the noose.

*   *   *

Chrissie Gall turned to drink as her shame over the lack of a marriage contract between herself and Peter Queen took hold. She had strong religious scruples and the fact that she and Peter, whom she loved dearly, were merely living in the guise of man and wife was too much for her to bear. The fear of her family discovering that she was living in sin drove her towards the bottle – and thoughts of suicide.

But thirty-one-year-old Peter, the son of wealthy Glasgow bookmaker Thomas Queen, could not marry her. For he was already wedded to another although the marriage was over. Curiously, his first wife had also been an alcoholic. He had married her in 1918 but the marriage lasted just two years before her drinking habits forced her into a sanatorium. The heartbroken man, now known as 'Poor Peter' by friends and relatives, returned to live with his family.

A certified nursemaid, Chrissie, four year younger than the man she loved, took up employment in the Queen household when she was around twenty years of age. However, this was no upstairs/downstairs affair for they did not become overly friendly until after she had left the job, eighteen months later. Her mother was seriously ill and she returned to the family home on Tollcross Road, in the east end of the city, to look after her shoemaker father, John. She and Peter kept in touch and romance, as they say, blossomed. Her father was a man of strict moral beliefs and, although he may have known his daughter was stepping out with the still-married Peter Queen, to his credit he did not force her to break it off. Chrissie had inherited some of his strict views but the heart wants what the heart wants and she continued to see Peter even though every nerve and sinew in her young body was screaming that it was wrong.

When her mother died, Chrissie remained to tend to her father and the love affair with Peter continued. But, three years later, John Gall decided to move in with one of his other daughters and Chrissie found herself homeless. Peter rode to the rescue, renting her lodgings with tram conductor James Burns and his wife Fay in Hayburn Street, Partick. Three months later, at Christmas, Peter moved in with her. This was 1930 and a couple living together without benefit of clergy was, like a glimpse of stocking in olden days, looked on as something shocking. Cole Porter might have been telling the world that anything goes but he was a rich American writing in New York. This was a Glasgow still in the grip of sharp-faced Presbyterianism. Ashamed, Chrissie kept her situation from her family. She told them she was back in service, in a live-in position. To keep up the pretence she even visited her sister and father once a week on a Wednesday, pretending that it was her half-day off.

But she had another secret that she kept from them. Chrissie had already shown a weakness for drink. Now her shame really began to take its toll on her delicate psyche and she used alcohol to blur the edges. But her strict moral upbringing was not to be washed away and, as she tried to drown her problems, they were learning to swim. Her drinking grew worse and Poor Peter must have wondered what he had done in a past life to merit the two women he loved becoming alcoholics.

Everyone agreed he did everything he could to help Chrissie through her troubles. He was supportive, he was sympathetic and he never seemed to lose his temper. There were quarrels, of course, mostly when Chrissie was demanding money to buy drink. But, when it was suggested that he walk away from her, Peter quietly stated, 'I will never give her up.'

Chrissie, though, grew worse. When she was depressed, she drank and, when she drank, she got more depressed. And with the drinking and the depression came the threats of suicide.

James Burns and his wife, in the thick of the drama, tried to help as much as they could. Fay Burns would hunt out the bottles Chrissie had hidden around the house and empty the contents down the sink. Each time, Chrissie promised meekly that she would stop drinking but, each time, she would break that promise. Sitting with Mrs Burns one day, drunk as usual, Chrissie suddenly leaped up and said she was going to 'make a hole in the Clyde' and dashed for the door. Her landlady hauled her back and calmed her down. Finally, she elicited a promise from the young woman that she would stop drinking. Chrissie managed to last a week before she came home rolling drunk yet again. A disappointed Mrs Burns upbraided her and Chrissie replied, 'It's all very well for you to speak that way but you don't understand. Some day, you will come in and find me strung up.'

Once Chrissie got up in the middle of the night and turned on the gas, ostensibly to boil a kettle, but did not light it. Then, drunk no doubt, she went to bed and left the gas hissing into the room. Had Mrs Burns not been awakened by the smell they could all have been killed. Whether this was a deliberate act or just a case of drunken absent-mindedness cannot be said but Peter did tell his friends the following day that he had been following her round all night switching off the gases.

In August 1931, Peter and Chrissie moved into their own rooms at 539 Dumbarton Road. By now Mrs Burns's sister, Helen Johnston, had got to know the couple and she had also tried to talk Chrissie into turning her back on the bottle. Chrissie promised and promised and promised but then her shame wagged its finger at her and she tried to still it with whisky and gin. And, as always, this led to depression and thoughts of death. She told Mrs Johnson that she'd take a double dose of medicine or that, one day, Peter would come home to find her hanging behind the door. But, the gas incident aside, they seemed to be merely threats – attempts at attention seeking perhaps – until the night she tried to hang herself.

On Thursday 12 November, James and Fay Burns called in at the Dumbarton Road flat for a cup of tea. James Burns went to hang his coat up behind the door when he noticed the hook was broken. 'Who's been breaking up the happy home?" he asked.

Peter Queen said Chrissie had tried to do herself in the night before. He had woken up in the middle of the night when he heard a noise. Later, in court, he outlined what he found. 'I could see no one about. I got up then and lit the gas and saw Chrissie sagging against the door with a rope tied around her neck. I immediately caught her up and took the rope from her neck. When I got her straightened up, she fell against me very much dazed. I got her back into bed and got some water.'

Chrissie told James and Fay Burns that she had been a damned fool. She knew the drinking was doing her harm and she was resolved to stop. And she did manage to stop – for two whole days. Around this time, James Burns's brother-in-law Leonard Johnson spoke to her, pleading with her to change her ways and that, if she didn't, it was going to kill her.

'I know,' she said, 'but you don't know the position I am in, having to maintain so much pretence. I am fed up with life. I have to tell lies everywhere I go. I cannot go home to my own people. Some day Peter will find me behind the door.'

It was decided that she might benefit from a week's holiday and Peter suggested Aberdeen. Chrissie was not too keen but she agreed, even arranging to take her ailing young niece with her. Peter thought that was a grand idea – looking after the youngster might take her mind off her problems – and arranged for lodgings. She was due to head north on Monday 23 November. But the much-needed vacation would never take place. For, within days of the decision being taken, Chrissie Gall was dead – and her loving 'husband' facing a capital murder charge.

On Thursday 19 November, Chrissie went on a monumental drinking binge. She had visited her father to tell him about her impending trip to the Granite City and later she had met up with her brother, Robert, a grocer. Whisky and beer were consumed and then Chrissie said she had to be going as she was due to meet Peter at 5.15 p.m. Bert Gall went with her and together they were drawn into a nearby pub where, naturally, more spirits were duly quaffed. Armed with a bottle of whisky, they headed off to catch a bus across the city to Dumbarton Road, where the aromatic pleasures of another pub lured them inside. However, noticing her advanced state of intoxication, the barman refused to serve Chrissie.

She and Bert left to weave their way to her flat. They arrived at around 9 p.m. to find a very anxious Peter Queen waiting for her. She told him she'd been at her sister's house and he seemed satisfied with that – although he was worried about her condition. It had been raining and her feet were soaking wet so he helped her take off her shoes and told her to warm herself in front of the fire.

Slowly, Chrissie's mind began to clear and with her sobriety came the realisation that this was the first time she had taken a relative back to the flat. Her family still did not know she and Peter were living as man and wife and as far as she was concerned they must never know. But here was her brother Bert and the man she called husband sitting together in their love nest. She scribbled a note to Peter and slipped it to him, telling him to pretend this was his aunt's flat. He quickly realised what she wanted him to do and he played his part to the full. He managed to get Bert out of the house and, as he was walking him to the tram stop, he said that Chrissie had a long way to get home and she should rest first. Bert seemed to accept it all without question. But he would never see his sister alive again.

Mrs Johnson found Chrissie in the flat the following day – alone and completely drunk. She was sure that her little charade the night before had failed to convince her brother and she was terrified he would tell the rest of the family that she was living with Peter Queen. The worried Mrs Johnson sent word to Peter, who was working as a clerk for his father's firm, saying that Chrissie was very ill and suggesting that he should come home in the early afternoon. It was also suggested that a doctor should be called but Peter could not get one to come that afternoon. He did, however, arrange for a home visit the following morning. Mrs Johnson returned later in the day with her husband and stayed for the rest of the evening. Chrissie had been asleep most of the time but did wake up at around 8.30 p.m. looking for a drink. She had to settle for some ginger ale and some hot water and sugar. Later she had tea and sandwiches before the Johnsons left at around 10.45 p.m.

When Peter told Chrissie that he'd arranged for the doctor to visit the following morning, she asked him to fetch the good pillowcases from the other room. He said he looked for around fifteen minutes but did not find the pillowcases. When he went back into the other room of the two-roomed flat, the curtains around their bed were drawn and he assumed Chrissie had gone back to sleep. He sat at the table for a while, smoking a cigarette, and then he went over to see how she was. When he drew back the curtain, he said, he got the shock of his life. His beloved Chrissie was lying in the bed, a rope tied tightly around her neck. Her face, the face he loved, was swollen, the tongue protruding from the mouth – the mouth he had kissed.

'I don't know what happened next,' he said in court. 'I must have collapsed or something. It knocked me out.'

Only two people knew exactly what happened in that small cramped room in that Glasgow tenement – and one of them was dead. We have only Peter Queen's version of events and the theories of the prosecution. However, what Queen did next would not help his assertion that Chrissie had somehow managed to strangle herself. He did not try to loosen the noose that was biting into her neck and nor did he try to alert a doctor. Instead, he rushed out of the flat and into the street where he met PC Alex McLeod walking his beat. PC McLeod said the man mentioned nothing about his wife being dead but merely asked for directions to the nearest police office. PC McLeod directed him to the Partick office, known locally as the Marine. It took Peter a few minutes to walk through the dark of night to the police office, finally arriving there at around 3 a.m. By now, he was extremely agitated. He threw his house keys on to the counter and told police that his wife was dead in their flat. Then came the fatal six words – six words that would hold the key to life and death for Peter Queen less than three months later. For his guilt or innocence depended on which version the jury believed.

The police version was that Peter Queen, on being asked what had happened, said, 'I think I have killed her.' If this was the case, it was a clear confession. Peter had his face buried in his hands as he spoke, the officers said, but, when he said the words, he looked up and his voice was perfectly clear.

Peter Queen, though, denied saying this. His version was that, when asked what happened, he replied, 'Don't think I have killed her.' – one word of a difference. It was a very subtle difference but a difference nonetheless. Where the police version was a confession, this was a denial. But the police had a major problem with their version. Although they were emphatic that the words had been spoken just as they stated, no one had thought to take a written record. Here was a man who was, apparently, confessing to murder. That confession was witnessed by at least two officers and yet not one of them had thought to write it down. In court, when being questioned about this very point, the police witnesses became very evasive and it wasn't until the trial judge, Lord Alness, asked them pointed questions was it admitted that no official record was kept.

Meanwhile, back on that November night, officers had arrived at the flat to find the light still burning in the death room. They found Chrissie Gall lying on her back, her face turned away. Her left arm was fully extended from the shoulder, her right one was under the covers, which were pulled up to her chest. Both her dressing jacket and boudoir cap were still in place. She looked peaceful, with no expression of pain. She looked asleep. But she wasn't asleep. There was a cord, cut from the kitchen pulley, tied round her neck in what appeared to be single knot. The flesh of the neck was broken, her face was discoloured, her eyes closed, her mouth slightly open, her tongue bulging slightly from beneath her teeth, the upper set, which were false, still in place. One of the officers loosened the tight noose although it was not as tight perhaps as the one awaiting Peter Queen who, within two hours, was formally charged with murdering Christine Robertson Gall.

'I have nothing to say,' he replied. And, this time, his words were carefully noted.

The Crown case was very simple. Peter Queen, tired of his lover's drinking, of her depressions, of her suicide threats, had finally

Picturesque Eaglesham, now a conservation village, has changed very little since Agnes Montgomery died in agony in a room in a house like one of these.

The village kirk at Eaglesham is where Agnes Montgomery was buried and then disinterred to allow doctors to search for poisons in her corpse.

A typical Victorian family portrait but this studied pose hid a dangerous secret –
Dr Edward Pritchard was plotting the deaths of his wife and his mother-in-law.

Calton Jail, Edinburgh, where Eugène Marie Chantrelle was executed and Dr
Edward Pritchard was held during his trial. Only the turreted governor's
residence remains today.

Yours truly,
E. Chantrelle.

NOTICE
IN REGARD TO THE TRIAL OF
EUGÈNE MARIE CHANTRELLE,
On TUESDAY, 7th MAY 1878.

1. No one, except Judges, to be introduced to the Bench, unless on application to the Court.

2. No one to be within the Bar except the Gentlemen engaged in the Case and the Faculty Reporter and his Assistant.

3. No one to be admitted at the Door on the West side of the Court opposite the Edinburgh Reporters' Seat except Reporters, and the Policemen will send in to the Reporters the Cards of their Messengers.

4. The Side Seat opposite the Jury Box to be kept for Reporters other than Edinburgh Reporters.

5. Advocates, W.S.'s, and S.S.C.'s, will enter by the Door immediately adjoining that of the Reporters.

6. The passage and side doors on the East of the Court are reserved for Crown Counsel, and for Crown Officials connected with the Case, and for the Jury after being Balloted.

7. No one to be allowed to stand in the Passages inside the Court.

8. Besides the Faculty Seat behind the Reporters' Seat, one of the Side Galleries to be kept, so far as necessary, for Advocates whose Officer will attend. It is expected that Advocates shall be in their Bar Dress, and that those only will take places in the Gallery who mean to attend for the day, as the private stair is so close to the Bench that going up and down disturbs the Judges.

9. Strict Orders are given that no Money be taken at the Doors for admission to any part of the Court.

10. The Doors will be opened at 10 o'clock.

11. A Policeman to be on the Outside and another on the Inside of each Door of the Court.

12. The Police to keep the Passages clear.

This photo of the magnificently whiskered Eugène Marie Chantrelle, who was considered handsome in his day, was taken around the time of his trial.

A contemporary notice detailing the special arrangements that were put in place during the trial of Eugène Marie Chantrelle's sensational trial.

The Safeway store at Hunter's Tryst, Edinburgh, where the bottles of tonic water that Dr Paul Agutter laced with poison were purchased.

Dr Paul Agutter being led away from court after being found guilty of attempting to poison his wife.

Beautiful Alice Hutchison who was brutally murdered by her husband at their villa in Spain.

The Hutchisons' Spanish villa

AUDIENCIA PROVINCIAL
SECCION 3ª

Stuart Hutchison being escorted into a Spanish courtroom
to face trial for the murder of his wife.

Workers at the Bothwell Bank
Sewage Works where the
remains of murdered George
Hall were discovered.

Bothwell Bank Sewage Works

George Carlin who felt so threatened by George Hall that he hired
someone to kill him. The hitman has never been caught.

snapped, cut a length of cord from the kitchen pulley with a kitchen knife and had strangled her. They had medical experts to support their case, including Professor John Glaister, the highly respected Chair of Forensic Medicine at the University of Glasgow, and Professor Andrew Allison, of St Mungo College, who carried out the post-mortem. Both men believed that Chrissie Gall's death was inconsistent with self-destruction. Professor Glaister summed up their view saying, 'Several factors exclude suicide. These include the attitude of the body, the position of the arms, the position of the ends of the ligature, the fracture of the cricoia and the degree of constriction.'

They believed Chrissie Gall would have fallen unconscious before sufficient pressure was brought on the noose to kill. Her grip would have then relaxed and her hands would then have fallen away from the ligature. Also, one of the arms was found under the bedclothes, while the cricoid cartilage – a round cartilage in the larynx – had been fractured. In their opinion, it would take tremendous pressure to crack this tough piece of gristle. 'The degree of force was fairly considerable and death would be rapid,' opined Professor Allison.

But, in Spilsbury and Smith, the defence had their own heavy-hitting forensic team – and they felt the opposite was possible, although one of the dynamic duo was not prepared to state with certainty that Chrissie Gall killed herself.

Sir Bernard Spilsbury was a legal legend. In English courts, it was said, his word was law and few juries questioned his judgement in a case. Along with Sir Sydney Smith, the eminent pathologist from Edinburgh University, he was hired by Queen's defence to look at the death of Chrissie Gall. It was the first and last time these two forensic giants would appear on the same side in a murder case.

From the beginning, Spilsbury was convinced Chrissie Gall had killed herself. There were no signs of a struggle in the room. The bed appeared undisturbed. Although the cricoid cartilage was cracked, there was none of the haemorrhaging or bruising on the deeper parts of the neck or thyroid he would expect to see in murder by strangulation when the killer generally keeps the pressure up on a tight ligature. The ligature itself was low down on the neck, with the half-knot just slightly to the right. He felt that, if it were murder, the ligature would have been higher up and the knot would have been further to the right. He doubted if a killer would use a half-knot for fear it might slip. Also, there was no sign of Chrissie scraping at the noose as it tightened on her throat, which might be expected if it was murder.

The Crown assertion that she would lose consciousness quickly and let go of the ligature was easily explained, Spilsbury thought. Under the microscope he saw that the fibres of the cord wove together under pressure and would have stayed in place, even after her hands fell away. However, there seemed to be no explanation as to how she did all this yet still have one arm under the bedclothes.

Although he did not believe Peter Queen killed the woman, Sir Sydney Smith did not feel the evidence was strong enough for him to say without any reservation that Chrissie Gall killed herself. He tended toward the suicide theory but he could not completely rule out the possibility of murder. In the end, it would be up to the jury to decide which version of Chrissie Gall's last moments was the truth.

The case was a sensation in Glasgow. Spectators packed the public gallery for the five-day trial, some queuing up from six in the morning to be sure of a seat. The unlucky ones milled about outside the courtroom, braving the January rain for a chance to witness such unusual proceedings. For the 'Murder or Suicide' case had caught their imagination.

The Crown presented their case first. Peter Queen had murdered Chrissie Gall because he had tired of her drinking and her depression. He had cut the cord from the pulley and strangled her as she lay in a drunken sleep. She did not know what was happening and that was why there were no signs of a struggle. However, the post-mortem failed to confirm the presence of alcohol in the stomach or blood – probably because the doctors performing it omitted to carry out the necessary tests.

They used the fact that Peter Queen failed to check for a pulse when he found the body, failed to fetch medical help and, the pièce de résistance, confessed to the police by saying, 'I think I have killed her.' True, the officers involved did not write that down at the time but that did not mean he did not say it.

A dramatic trial was made even more sensational by the collapse of one of the expert witnesses in the box. Professor Allison had a serious dose of the flu and, while being cross-examined by the defence, his face visibly paled and he pitched forward. Defence counsel R McGregor Mitchell saw him sway and was the first to his side, catching the man and helping him to a seat. Professor John Glaister and Sir Sydney Smith were among the medical men who treated him. The trial was adjourned for the day but the forty-eight-year-old professor had recovered sufficiently to resume his evidence the following day.

The defence hammered away at the suicide theory. Chrissie Gall had suicidal tendencies, even the prosecution's own witnesses confirmed that. Peter Queen had shown nothing but love, support and tenderness towards her – something that was, again, confirmed by the prosecution's own witnesses. So, according to the eminent pathologist Sir Bernard Spilsbury, supported to an extent by Scotland's own Sir Sydney Smith, she had killed herself.

Peter Queen opted to take the stand and spoke for five hours about his life with Chrissie and his shock at finding her dead in bed that terrible November night. He spoke emotionally about taking her in his arms and crying out, 'Chris, Chris, speak to me.' The strain of reliving that night was evident. As he spoke his body swayed, a nerve jumped in his face and his eyes were tightly closed, 'as if he was trying to shut out the memory of the scene,' wrote one journalist.

He insisted the police version of his initial statement was wrong. He was asked in court, 'When you were asked what was the matter, what did you say?'

'I said, "My wife is dead. Don't think I have killed her.".'

'What gave you the idea that there was any question of killing?'

'They kept on asking me what was the matter. I thought I might be blamed. That is why I said, "Don't think I have killed her.".'

He denied he had tired of Chrissie although he did admit he was very worried about the route their life was taking. 'The impression she gave me,' he said, 'was that it was due to her living with me – to the fact that her people might get to know about us.' And he firmly denied strangling her to be rid of a woman who had become a drain on him both financially and emotionally.

'I put it to you,' accused the advocate depute, 'that what really happened that night is that you, with a bread knife, cut the end of the pulley rope.'

'I did not,' said Queen.

'And strangled her,' he continued.

'I did not.'

Finally, as it always must, it all came down to what the jury believed. The nine women and six men left the courtroom at around 3.30 p.m. on Saturday 9 January, to consider their verdict. For two hours, they disputed and debated and discussed. For two hours, they argued whether the prosecution's expert witnesses were more expert than those that the defence had produced. For two hours, they talked over the true nature of Queen's statement to the police. Was it a confession or a denial?

At 5.30 p.m., the bell rang to alert all interested parties that the jury had reached a decision. The judges, the lawyers, the witnesses, the spectators, the journalists and, more importantly, the accused all filed back into the court to hear the dread news. Peter Queen stood in the dock, his face pale and his body stiff, as he waited to hear his fate. His father sat beside the dock, his face tense. The two men – and everyone else in the courtroom – watched as the jury took their places and the forewoman was asked for their verdict on the charge of murder. The woman could not speak but the handkerchief that fluttered to her face to dab at the tears spoke volumes. It was left to a male juror to speak out. 'Guilty, my Lord,' he said in a clear voice. A sigh breathed through the room and somewhere a woman cried out.

Queen, rigid now as he stood to face the judges, knew in his heart there was only one punishment under law for the crime of murder. The jury had reached a majority verdict and had lodged a strong plea for clemency but Lord Alness had no choice – he had to sentence thirty-one-year-old Peter Queen to death. In a trembling voice, the judge decreed that he would hang in Duke Street Prison on 30 January.

Peter Queen's head bobbed slightly as he turned, picked up the hat from where he had left it on the bench behind him and was led to the cells below. His father, tears brimming in his eyes, stretched his hands through the bars around the dock but could not reach his son.

It was the longest trial in Glasgow for decades and the first in thirty years to be concluded on a Saturday. There was an appeal, of course, but it failed and the execution date was duly amended to Saturday 13 February. But the jury's wish for mercy was echoed in a petition signed by 400 of the city's leading politicians and citizens. And the powers-that-be listened. Just after breakfast on 10 February, Peter Queen received a visitor in his cell. It was Glasgow's Lord Provost Sir Thomas Kelly and he had come bearing a letter from the Secretary of State for Scotland authorising the sentence to be commuted to penal servitude for life.

On his release some years later, Queen returned to Glasgow to begin his life again and took a job as a bookmaker's clerk. He made new friends but few of them knew of his past. He died in 1958 in happy obscurity.

7

WHO LOVES MOST
Buck Ruxton

The three sisters had come to the seaside resort to see the spectacle. They came every year in September to wonder at the bright lights and to be amazed by the splendour that modern technology could create. The lights sparkled in the dark of the night. They winked at their own reflection shimmering on the sea's black surface. They hung on Blackpool's landmark Tower like a string of twinkling beads. The sights and the sounds and the ambience of the Lancashire town, as usual, amazed the women. They were Scots and somehow the lure of Blackpool has always proved a strong one for that particular nation. But the day, as all days must, reached its end and it was time for one of their number to return home. She lived in Lancaster to the north and she had only come through for the day. At 11.30 p.m., she climbed into her husband's Hillman Minx car and bade goodbye to the remaining two. As she left, she promised to return the following day and then they drove off, the lights of the car merging and finally disappearing among the countless others glittering through the night.

But these three sisters would never meet again.

On Sunday 29 September 1935, Susan Haines Johnson, from Lenzie, north of Glasgow, was on holiday in Moffat, a picturesque town in what is now Dumfries and Galloway. About two miles north of the town is Gardenholme Linn, a small stream that tumbles through a ravine towards the River Annan. The stream is crossed by the Edinburgh to Carlisle road by means of a bridge and Miss Johnson was on this bridge, admiring the view and watching the water cascading over the rocks below, when she noticed a curious package lying beneath her. It was not the package itself that was curious, it was what appeared to be sticking out of it that caught her eye. It looked, from her vantage point, like a human arm.

An ashen-faced Miss Johnson returned quickly to the Moffat hotel that she was staying in and told her brother Charles what she had seen. Together they made their way back to the bridge over the gully and the macabre bundle. Charles climbed down as far as he could for a closer inspection and confirmed that it was, indeed, a human arm. But it did not end there, for he could see a further four packages nearby. Shinning back up the side of the ravine, the Johnson siblings sped back again to Moffat to alert the police. A Sergeant Sloan was the first man on the scene and he gingerly opened the bundles to reveal their grisly contents.

The body parts were wrapped in a variety of items, including a bed sheet, a child's woollen romper suit, a blouse and pages from newspapers *The Sunday Graphic*, *Daily Herald* and *Sunday Chronicle*. There were arms and legs and feet and pieces of flesh, all hacked from the body. There were two heads. And there was a piece of a human torso.

The shocking discovery sparked a full-scale search and, over the next month, a total of thirty packages were found in the area. The final tally of body parts reached seventy, including the two human heads, two sections of human trunks, seventeen limbs and over forty pieces of 'soft tissue', including three female breasts, two portions of external female sex organs and a uterus. Curiously, there was also a Cyclops eye – a specimen where, due to a malformation of the skull and brain, two eyes merge into one – found among the fleshy items although this proved to be something of a red herring. It was later assumed to have been a surgical specimen that had somehow made its way into the bundles.

The bodies had been dissected with some surgical skill and all means of identifying them had been removed – facial features had been scraped away, fingers and thumbs had been severed, teeth had been pulled, heads had been scalped. The killer no doubt believed he had committed the perfect murders by mutilating his two victims in such a fashion. He would have been convinced that tracing the victims back to him was nigh on impossible. But, although it is said there are only two things that are certain in this life – death and taxes – there is, in fact, a third. And that is that nothing is perfect.

Bakhtyar Rustomji Ruttonju Hakim was a doctor and a well-respected one at that. He was a Parsee. Parsees adhere to Zoroastrianism, one of the world's oldest religions which is now in decline due to strict rules that forbid marriage with other faiths. The word Parsee is derived from the word Persian and it was from there that the followers of the Iranian prophet Zoroaster fled around 1,000 years ago. They settled in India and thrived, becoming wealthy, educated and socially aware. Bombay-born Bakhtyar Hakim was a fine example of the Parsee tradition. He qualified in medicine at both his home university and in London. He was also a Bachelor in Surgery at the University of Bombay although he did fail the exam for fellowship of the prestigious Royal College of Surgeons in Edinburgh. Serving with the Indian Medical Service, he practised his skills in the Iraqi cities of Basra and Baghdad before arriving in London, where he worked for a time.

By 1927, he was in Edinburgh, studying for a post-graduate degree in medicine. Then, using the name Captain Gabriel Hakim, the twenty-nine-year-old doctor frequented a restaurant in Princes Street, managed by a Mrs Isabella Van Ness. She was two years younger than her exotic regular customer and had married a Dutch seaman eight years earlier. However, the marriage had failed after only a fortnight and was annulled in Holland. She then reverted to using her maiden name of Kerr. Romance blossomed between the two and, the following year, she gave up her job and joined him in London where he was then practising. Two years later they settled as man and wife in Lancaster. However, they were never formally married for, although Isabella's marriage had been legally terminated, Bakhtyar Hakim – who had by now changed his name by deed poll to the more Anglo-friendly Buck Ruxton – already had a Parsee wife back home in Bombay. At any rate, his religion forbade any such union.

Dr Ruxton had bought a practice based in a three-storey, twelve-room terraced house at 2 Dalton Square in the old Roman town. They had three children together and were as devoted to them as any parents could be. They hired twenty-year-old local girl Mary Jane Rogerson to help look after the children. They also had two other 'servants' – women who came in to help with the household duties. But things between the couple were tempestuous to say the least. As Ruxton himself later said, 'We were the kind of people who could not live with each other and could not live without each other.' He also quoted a French proverb which translates as 'Who loves most chastises most.'.

Some of that chastisement reared its head during his frequent outbursts of jealousy. Ruxton was convinced his wife was unfaithful. Even the sight of her talking to another man could ignite his rage and this, in turn, could lead to him beating the woman he professed to love. Sometimes things would reach such a stage that Isabella felt her life was in danger and, on at least two occasions, she turned to the police for help. Police officers claimed that he often acted like a wild man and threatened to kill her. 'I would be justified in murdering her,' he is alleged to have said on one occasion while, on another, it was, 'My wife has been unfaithful and I will kill her if it continues.'

One former maid, Scot Eliza Hunter, from Holytown in Lanarkshire, said that, on one occasion, Mrs Ruxton left her husband. The maid said that the doctor then told her that his wife 'won't come back alive. I will bring her back to the mortuary.' On another occasion, Eliza said she heard Isabella crying out for help and she found the doctor holding his wife down by the throat. He turned on her when she appeared and told her it was none of her business.

Despite the wild accusations and the violent fits of temper, despite his sleeping with a revolver under his pillow and despite reports by witnesses of his holding a knife at Isabella's throat, the couple never separated for long. Once she ran home to mother in Edinburgh but Ruxton followed her and begged her to return to him. And, in 1932, one of her sisters was summoned urgently to Lancaster after being told by Ruxton that Isabella had tried to gas herself. It was not the first time she had attempted suicide, he claimed, and accused her of trying to ruin him.

Then, in September 1935, matters reached a climax.

The body parts were removed to a small mortuary in Moffat's cemetery. Following an examination in situ by Professor John Glaister, Regius Professor of Forensic Medicine at the University of Glasgow, and Dr Gilbert Miller, Lecturer in Pathology at Edinburgh University, the remains were gathered together and shipped off to the latter university's anatomy department for closer scrutiny under the direction of Professor J C Brash. Professor Sydney Smith, Regius Professor of Forensic Medicine at Edinburgh, and Dr Arthur Hutchinson, Dean of the Edinburgh Dental Hospital and School, completed the crack forensic squad. Professors Glaister and Smith had been on opposite sides during the Peter Queen case but here they were on the same team.

The scientists had something of a jigsaw puzzle on their hands – and by no means a complete one. Their first task was to work out just how many bodies they were dealing with. After studying the various body parts rescued from the area around Moffat, they realised that there were two. At first, it was believed one was male and one was female – a fact duly passed on to a salivating press pack. But, as the pieces of the puzzle were slowly brought together, hip bones connecting to thigh bones, thigh bones connecting to knee bones, they heard the word of the Lord and that word was that they were wrong about one of the bodies – dead wrong.

They worked out that they had, in fact, the remains of two females which, in the absence of any other identification, they named somewhat prosaically Body No 1 and Body No 2. They only had one pelvis. It fitted Body No 2 and it was obviously female. Body No 1 took some medical detective work. Although the head had been scalped, some hair fragments remained and they suggested the person was female. There was no sign of a beard and the larynx was small. The trunk of Body No 1 was completely missing but what they had of the body suggested that the person was small, between four feet ten inches and five feet, and had the rounded, slender limbs of a female. But what clinched it was that among the fleshy parts found were three female breasts. Once they had worked out they were working with only two bodies, it was then obvious that both were female.

The victims' sex had now been determined so the team now turned to establishing age. Bones and skulls take on different characteristics as a person grows older and, using X-rays, they estimated that Body No 1 was aged between eighteen and twenty-five while Body No 2 was aged between thirty-five and forty-five. A dental examination of Body No 1 revealed that there were wisdom teeth that had not yet come through, so the age was pegged at around twenty.

The killer had dismembered the bodies to make disposal easier. However, he had also performed certain mutilations that may have had a purpose other than the gratification of his blood lust. The eyes of both bodies had been removed, as had the nose, lips, ears and most of the facial skin. Some teeth had been pulled from both. The flesh of the right thumb on Body No 1 had been peeled off while, similarly, part of the right arm had been stripped of its skin. Body No 2 had the ends of the fingers cut off and flesh had been sliced from the legs and cut away from part of the left foot. This was no mere butchery. There was method in this madness. But, before the scientists could understand why it was done, they would need to know who the victims were.

By the beginning of September, Buck Ruxton's insane jealousy was plumbing new depths. On 7 September 1935, his wife planned to go on a trip to Edinburgh with the Edmondson family with whom she had become friendly. However, the doctor had convinced himself there was something going on between Isabella and young Robert Edmondson, who worked for Lancaster Council. The original plan had been for them to drive north in two cars and Isabella would stay with her sister in Edinburgh. But, for some reason, that plan changed and, instead, they all took rooms in Edinburgh's Adelphi Hotel. Ruxton, who had hired another car and followed them all the way, was furious. That they had stayed overnight in a hotel – despite the fact that there was never any definite proof that there was any sort of affair in progress – was enough for him. In his mind, Isabella was sleeping with young Edmondson.

Unusually for him, given his volatile temperament, he did not burst into the hotel, screaming his accusations, but waited until she returned home before confronting her. He made his now customary wild reproaches and she denied them. Perhaps, after it all, they made up in their normal passionate way. But the following week, on 14 September, Isabella set off in the car again, this time heading south on her annual pilgrimage to see the illuminations at Blackpool with her two sisters. Ruxton knew she was going but could not shake off his dark jealousies. In his fevered mind she was not going to Blackpool to see the lights, she was going to meet *him*, she was going to see *him*, she was going to sleep with *him*.

She would only be gone a day but that was long enough for him to sit at home and stew; long enough for him to imagine her walking hand in hand along the sparkling promenade with the younger man; long enough to visualise them locked in a naked embrace in some seafront hotel. When she came home that night, he would have resolved to have it out with her once and for all.

While the medical detectives were working wonders in Edinburgh, Scottish police were conducting their own painstaking investigation in an attempt to track the killer. The initial fear was that there was some sort of maniac at large in Britain, for there had been other dismembered bodies found in Brighton and London. However, a link to these other crimes was soon discounted. They knew the women had been murdered and mutilated elsewhere before being dumped in the ravine. They knew the packages had been disposed of some time between 15 September and 19 September. Both the Gardenholme Linn and the River Annan had been in spate following heavy rainfalls on 17 and 18 September and some of the bundles had been carried downstream before being left high but far from dry as the water level subsided. A car had no doubt been used to transport the body parts but no one saw a strange car on the bridge over the Gardenholme Linn.

They examined the items that had been wrapped round the body parts. The edition of the *Sunday Graphic* newspaper, dated 15 September, was of particular interest. It was a 'slip edition' – a special limited print concerning the recent Morecambe Carnival and was available only in the Morecambe/Lancaster area. On 9 October, the Chief Constable of Dumfries contacted his opposite number in Lancaster Borough, asking for assistance. This may have been the break they were looking for – but, on the same day, another newspaper was to provide the first real link to the murdered women. The Dumfries police chief was shown an item in that day's *Daily Record* concerning the disappearance of a young woman three weeks previously. Her name was Mary Jane Rogerson. She was from Lancaster. She was employed as the nursemaid to the family of Dr Buck Ruxton.

And Mrs Ruxton was also missing.

At 6.30 a.m. on Sunday 15 September, the husband of charlady Mrs Agnes Oxley opened his front door to an unexpected visitor – his wife's employer Dr Buck Ruxton. Mrs Oxley usually went to the Ruxton house at just after 7 a.m. every day but this day the doctor told her that she should not 'trouble to come down this morning'. He added that Mrs Ruxton and Mary had gone away on a holiday to Edinburgh and concluded by saying, 'I am taking the children to Morecambe.'

At just after nine, a girl delivering newspapers to the Ruxton house was met by the doctor at the door. He held his right hand against his body, as if he was holding up his trousers, even though he was wearing braces. A woman delivering milk also saw him that morning. He told both that his wife and maid were away in Scotland. A third person called at the house that morning, making another newspaper delivery, this time the *Sunday Graphic*. Later that morning, Dr Ruxton visited a garage and bought four gallons of petrol in two two-gallon cans. He then visited another garage, his regular one, and had four gallons of petrol fed into his car. By 11 a.m., he was back home and a woman arrived for a small operation on her son. To her he said, 'I am sorry but I cannot perform the operation today as my wife is away in Scotland and there is just myself and my little maid and we are busy taking the carpets up ready for the decorators in the morning. Look at my hands, how dirty they are.' However, all the woman could see was his left hand as the doctor kept his right one hidden behind the door.

At midday, he deposited his three young children with a family friend, saying his wife and Mary Rogerson had gone away for a few days. The woman noticed that his right hand was injured and he explained he'd cut it on a tin of peaches he'd been opening for the children's breakfast. He then went home and was alone there until around 4.30 p.m. when he called on one of his patients, a Mrs Hampshire, saying that his wife was in Blackpool and Mary was on holiday. He had hurt his hand that morning and was unable to get the house ready for the decorators who were due to come the following day. He asked Mrs Hampshire if she would come and help him. She agreed and went back to Dalton Square with him. The woman's husband later joined them.

Mrs Hampshire found the carpets had been lifted from both the stairs and the upstairs landing and straw thrown down onto the dirty floors. She also saw straw poking out from under the doors to the bedrooms of Dr Ruxton and his wife. However, both doors were locked – the only doors in the house to be locked. There were carpets rolled up in the study and others stacked in the back yard. One carpet was stained with blood and also there were a bloodstained shirt and some partly burned towels. Ruxton said the blood was his – from his cut hand – and that he'd tried to burn them but they had proved too wet. He had even thrown petrol over them but had been unable to ignite them. He said the Hampshires could have the stair carpet and the underlay, as well as a blue suit that was bloodstained. He left them a key so that they could lock up after they were finished and then he went out. They cleaned up as best they could but Mrs Hampshire could not completely remove a stain that extended the length of the bath and up to six inches from the top. They also found what might have been blood on the bathroom linoleum and they managed to scrub this off. When they left, they took the suit and the carpets from the house that the doctor had offered them. However, they left the carpets in the yard as it had rained that afternoon and they were soaking wet.

The following day a haggard Buck Ruxton called again at their house. He had obviously thought better of giving Mr Hampshire the suit for he asked if they would return it – ostensibly so that he could have it cleaned. Mrs Hampshire said she would get it cleaned herself so Ruxton had to content himself with making sure she cut off the name tab he had sewn into the sleeve and watching her burn it. After he left, the woman's suspicions were finally aroused and she took a closer look at the garment. The waistcoat was so covered in blood that it was unredeemable so she burned it. She then looked at the stair carpet and found it, too, was soaked with blood. She took it outside where, she said later, she threw between twenty to thirty buckets of water over it but it was never properly clean. The water streaming off was red with blood.

Mrs Oxley, the charlady, reported for work as normal the next morning to find the house locked and no answer to the doorbell. She went home again and returned at just after nine, when the doctor arrived in his car. He let her in and she helped him bandage his hand. She busied herself with cleaning until lunchtime when

111

Mrs Hampshire arrived again. Later that day, Ruxton told Mrs Hampshire that his wife had gone off with another man. 'You make a friend of a man,' he said, 'you treat him as a friend and he eats at your table and he makes love to your wife behind your back.' He began to cry and said he could never forgive infidelity. However, he soon composed himself and was able to attend to some patients in his surgery.

Later that day, Ruxton's Hillman Minx was due for a service so he hired a four-seater Austin 12 saloon to use while it was in the garage. The registration number was CP 8415 – the same registration as a car involved in a hit and run in Kendal at lunchtime the following day, Tuesday 17 September. No one was hurt in the accident although a bicycle was badly damaged and, when police caught up with him, Ruxton said he'd been to Carlisle on business.

Whether he knew it or not, the doctor was acting very suspiciously at this time. The bottoms of curtains on the top landing were bloodstained and he tore the stained parts off and burned them in the fire. He was up most of the night burning something in his back yard and neighbours said the blaze was bright enough to read by. On Thursday 19 September, he said he was going to visit a specialist about his hand but made sure his charlady was in the kitchen with the door locked before he made several trips to his car, which was parked at the back door. When he was gone, the doors that previously had been locked were now open and there was a curious smell around the house. He also changed his story concerning his wife's disappearance, saying that she was in London not Edinburgh.

However, as time went on, the police were convinced she was in neither city.

It was Mary's stepmother who had contacted the press about the girl's disappearance. As soon as the Dumfries police chief saw the news item, he contacted Lancaster police again for a description of the missing maid. He also arranged for photographs of the blouse and child's rompers found wrapped round some of the body parts to be published. Mrs Rogerson said the blouse was her step-daughter's – she recognised a patch she had sewn under one arm – and the rompers were identified by a woman who had given them to Mary Rogerson for the Ruxton children.

Ruxton had told Mrs Rogerson that a laundry boy had been paying attention to Mary and had got her in the family way. His wife had taken Mary away to put the trouble right. Mr Rogerson did not believe the story and gave Ruxton an ultimatum – either his daughter was back by Sunday or he'd go to the police. The doctor begged him not to inform the authorities and promised Mary would be back soon. A week later, Ruxton told them that his wife and Mary had broken into his safe and stolen £30. He did not know where they had gone but said they would be back when the money ran out. The Rogersons, unconvinced by the doctor's changing stories, finally reported Mary's disappearance to the police.

As time went on, people began to talk, as people always do. And police officers, despite what they might like us to think, can talk as much as anyone. Reporters soon got wind of a possible connection between the two missing women and the bodies in the ravine. Ruxton, in his now usual excitable manner, complained to the Chief Constable of Lancaster, saying, 'This publicity is ruining my practice – particularly at a time when I am negotiating a loan on it.' He wanted police to publish a statement that there was no connection between the two cases. Naturally, they could not do that but they did manage to mollify the irate doctor.

Matters were further complicated by another murder – that of a Mrs Smalley in Morecambe. Police had been interviewing a number of people in connection with the case, including someone who worked for Dr Ruxton. Again Ruxton complained to the police about this and said that some people were saying he had killed the woman. He said that someone would put a dead baby on his doorstep and say he had killed it next. He was told that the police could do nothing about the press or local rumours – and then he was asked for a photograph of his wife. He provided one and gave them permission to release it to the press.

With that in hand, the scientific detectives were about to make investigative history.

With two possible victims now named, the forensic team beavered away in Edinburgh to match up what they had deduced from the bodies with known facts. Body No 1 was estimated to be twenty years of age – the same age as Mary Jane Rogerson. By measuring the length of bones they had and using a specially prepared formula, they believed the height of the person to have been between four feet ten inches and five feet – Mary was five feet tall. Mary had suffered badly from tonsillitis – the scientists had discovered evidence in the remains consistent with tonsillitis. Mary had four vaccination marks on her left arm – so did Body No 1. They took a cast of the body's left foot – it fitted one of Mary's shoes. Mary's hair was light brown – so were the samples from Body No 1. But there were further clues the killer had tried to cover up – although all he did, in the end, was draw attention to them. Mary was known to have had an operation on a septic right thumb and this had left a small scar – the killer had stripped the flesh on Body No 1's right thumb away. Mary had livid birthmarks on her right arm around the elbow – the killer had cut away the flesh from the right arm around the elbow.

Body No 2 had an estimated age of between thirty-five and forty-five – when she disappeared, Isabella Ruxton was just under thirty-five. Body No 2, which was more or less complete, measured five feet three inches – Isabella was just over five feet five inches. The missing woman's hair was mid brown – so was the hair found on the body. A cast of Body No 2's left foot fitted one of Isabella's shoes. But, again, it was what had been removed from the remains that spoke volumes. Isabella had very distinctive fingernails – they were curved, brittle and regularly manicured – and the fingertips of Body No 2 had been sliced off. She was described as having thick ankles with calves the same thickness all the way up to her knees – the flesh had been removed from both legs. Isabella had what were described as 'humped' toes – toes that are bent downwards, probably as a result of wearing shoes that were too small – and the toes of the single foot recovered from Body No 2 had been removed. Isabella had suffered from a bunion on her right toe – skin and tissue had been removed from the foot right down to the bone. The bridge of her nose had been uneven; the nose, along with other facial features, had been removed – but doctors said the bone and cartilage were arched.

Thanks to the maggots that had infested the remains, they were even able to establish a rough time of death. Dr Alexander Mearns of the Institute of Hygiene at the University of Glasgow studied the life cycle of the larvae found on the corpses and established that the bodies had been lying in the ravine since shortly after the last time Mary and Isabella were last seen alive. His work was groundbreaking in its day but it was not the only piece of pioneering forensic detection connected to the case. Armed with photographs of both women, the scientists set about using the skulls, now totally denuded of the remaining putrefying flesh, to help, once and for all, establish their identities.

The studio portrait of Isabella, provided by Ruxton, was blown up to life size. Skull No 2 was also photographed from a variety of angles in an attempt to match the position of the face in the portrait. The skull shots were then superimposed on to the portrait shot – and they fitted. A similar exercise was conducted on Skull No 1 although the photographs supplied of Mary Rogerson were not of such good quality. However, the overlay of the skull shot did appear to match. This was the first time such a technique had been employed in a murder case. The process could not, by itself, prove Bodies Nos 1 and 2 were Mary and Isabella but, when considered along with the long list of similar characteristics, it did go a long way to establishing the victims' identities.

Now all police needed to do was bring their killer to justice.

As time went on, Buck Ruxton grew twitchy. He knew his name had been put in the frame for the murders – he had commented on it to a number of people, including police officers – but, instead of laying low and hoping the dust would settle, he continually complained to police officers about interference in his affairs. He also tried to convince some potential witnesses that he was innocent, even going so far as asking some of them to say what they knew to be false. For instance, he asked Mrs Oxley to say that she had come round to the house on the Sunday after his wife disappeared whereas, in fact, he had called at her house early that morning to specifically tell her not to come. He asked another to say that he had been at her house on 19 September, when the truth was he had been nowhere near it on that day.

When he became aware that he was under suspicion, Ruxton began compiling a document, headed 'My Movements', detailing the period between 14 and 30 September. On Saturday 12 October, he was interviewed by officers from Scotland and Lancaster and asked if he could account for his movements in that period. He replied, 'I shall be only too pleased to tell you all that I can.' and promptly produced his makeshift journal. He made a statement, which he signed, and remained in police custody while other questions were put to him. At 7.20 , the following morning he was arrested and formally charged with the murder of Mary Rogerson. It was a few weeks later, while still being held on remand, that he was charged with the murder of Isabella Ruxton.

In the meantime, police were able to go through the house at 2 Dalton Square with a scientific fine-tooth comb. Professor John Glaister came down from Glasgow to oversee the operation and his team found bloodstains on floors, doors and walls as well as blood traces and tiny particles of flesh in the bath and drains. A segment of a cotton bed sheet found around one of the bundles in Scotland was compared with a sheet on a bed and was found not only to have come from the same loom but the same warp on that loom.

Glasgow policeman Detective Lieutenant Hammond also visited the Lancaster house in the days following Ruxton's arrest. Investigators were determined to leave no stone unturned in their attempts to prove the identities of the two bodies. Fingerprints had been taken from the left hand of Body No 1 and they were found to match prints in the house. The detective also discovered what he thought were two prints of Mary's right thumb in the house but, because the actual thumb had not been recovered at that time, it was impossible to compare them. However, on 4 November, the thumb was found – although it was in a greatly putrefied state. The epidermis – the outer skin – had completely rotted away, leaving only a portion of the dermis or underlying skin. However, it is on the dermis that the loops and ridges that make up an individual's fingerprints are to be found. The detective doggedly laboured until he had managed to obtain a dermal print from the decayed thumb – and they matched the two prints he had spotted in the house. Both John Glaister and Sydney Smith later said this was the first time in the UK that such dermal prints were used to identify a murder victim.

The trial began at Manchester Assizes on 2 March 1936. For complex legal reasons, Ruxton was, by now, only facing the charge of murdering Isabella. He was defended by Norman Birkett who would later sit on the bench during the Nuremberg Trials of Nazi officials. Over 100 witnesses were called, two hundred exhibits were employed and the accused himself fired off over 100 notes to his counsel during the case. Thanks to the Scottish forensic team and some solid detective work, the prosecution case was a strong one. The bloody carpets, the stained suit, the witnesses to Ruxton's jealous outbursts, the changing stories, the physical evidence linking the bodies in the ravine to the house in Dalton Square, all proved to be too powerful for the experienced barrister to combat – although he made a game attempt.

In the end, the only thing he could do, in terms of defending his client, was to put Ruxton on the stand – and that proved to be something of a poisoned chalice. At first, Ruxton was nervous and more than once appeared on the verge of tears but, as the examination progressed, he seemed to warm to his role. He admitted he and his wife argued but that afterwards their relationship was 'more than intimate'. He denied ever saying he would kill her if she were unfaithful, saying that the thought of it 'made his blood wild'. He claimed he did not kill his wife or the maid. 'It is a deliberate fantastic story,' he said. 'You might just as well say the sun was rising in the west and setting in the east.

He said his wife had returned from Blackpool that Saturday night and had gone to bed. The following morning she announced she was going to Edinburgh a day earlier than planned and that Mary was going with her. The two women, he said, left at between 9.15 a.m. and 9.30 a.m. – and he never saw them again. The blood found in the house was his not theirs. He had cut himself trying to open the tin of fruit for the children's breakfast. The blood had streamed from his hands as he went up the stairs to the bathroom to clean it. The blood on the suit he gave to Mr Hampshire was the accumulation of months of dealing with wounds in the course of his work.

However, under cross-examination by the prosecution, Ruxton's carefully controlled poise began to crumble. He could not answer difficult questions. He became emotional. His temper began to fray. At one point he erupted with, 'This is a court to give men justice not to put a man on the gallows for nothing.'

Ruxton gave his evidence over two days. It has been observed that if the case had ended on the first day of his testimony, the jury may well have given him the benefit of doubt and acquitted him. But his demeanour and anger on the second day worked against him. Norman Birkett gave an impassioned plea on his client's behalf. 'Suspicion is not enough,' he said, 'doubt is not enough, the accusing finger is not enough, the imaginative reconstructions of my learned friend are not enough.' But they were enough. At the end of the eleven-day trial, the jury took only an hour to find Buck Ruxton guilty of murdering his wife. Before the judge, Mr Justice Singleton, passed sentence, Ruxton was asked if he had anything to say and, naturally, the garrulous doctor declined to pass up the opportunity to hear his own voice. He raised his hand to the bench in a Roman salute and then said, 'I want to thank everybody for the patience and fairness of my trial. I should like to hear whatever his Lordship has to say about it.' The judge fixed the black cap on his head and sentenced him to death.

On the night before his execution, as he sat in his cell in Manchester's Strangeways Prison, Ruxton scribbled a note to Norman Birkett. He thanked the barrister for everything he had done, telling him he had left him 'a trivial token' in his will. This turned out to be a set of silver knives and forks, which Mr Birkett did not accept. Ruxton's note continued, 'I am leaving three bonnie little mites behind. If you can, please do be good to them. They are intelligent and good looking.' He hoped his son would become a doctor like his father and that his daughters would become nurses. The kindly and fair-minded Norman Birkett ensured the three Ruxton orphans were well taken care of afterwards.

The note to Birkett was not the only one Ruxton wrote. There was another letter, written earlier, that was infinitely more dramatic. It had been composed on the day after his arrest in Lancaster and handed, in a sealed envelope, to a *News of the World* reporter who visited him. 'Take great care of this,' said the doctor. 'They have charged me with murder and I, in turn, charge you to place this envelope in safety and security. On no account must it be opened until my death, if to die I am. If I am acquitted – and I think I must be acquitted – you will give it back to me.'

Despite the horrific nature of his crimes, 6,000 people signed a petition for a reprieve. The plea was refused and Ruxton received the news in the condemned cell with what was described as a 'fatalistic calm'. Home Office rules insisted that the executioner be in the prison by 4 p.m. on the day before a hanging so Thomas Pierrepoint, part of a family firm of hangmen, had to stay overnight in Strangeways Prison. This meant that he did not have to force his way through the anti-capital-punishment demonstrations taking place outside the prison. The demonstrations resulted in one noted campaigner being arrested. Mrs Van Der Elst found herself in the middle of a hostile crowd when she arrived on Tuesday 12 May 1936 to protest at the punishment being meted out to Buck Ruxton within the prison walls. She was met with jeers from the people as she told them that the doctor should not be hanged. Police finally charged her with breach of the peace and driving her motor car in a manner likely to threaten life and limb.

At 9 a.m., the crowd hushed as they waited for the prison bell to toll – that would be the signal that Tom Pierrepoint had done his job. But the bell did not toll. Instead, a notice was pinned to the prison gates to say that Ruxton had gone to his doom.

On the same day, the sealed envelope he had given to the reporter was handed to the *News of the World* editor and subsequently published. It read, 'I killed Mrs Ruxton in a fit of temper because I thought she had been with a man. I was mad at the time. Mary Rogerson was present at the time. I had to kill her.' The letter, short and far from sweet, was signed 'B. Ruxton'.

Unsubstantiated rumours hinted that he received £3,000 for the confession and that the money went towards paying his defence costs.

So, what happened on that Saturday night after Isabella returned home from Blackpool? No one can say for certain but, by piecing together scientific evidence and adding a little guesswork, we can come up with a likely scenario.

Whether or not he had planned finally to kill his wife we cannot say but we do know that Ruxton had the full day to build up a jealous rage. When Isabella returned that night they would have argued. As his anger turned to violence, Ruxton attacked her and strangled her – this was borne out by the medical evidence of a fractured hyoid bone in the throat of Body No 2, a swollen tongue and congestion of the brain and the condition of the lungs. The later removal of certain body parts, like the nose, the eyes and the lips, could have been an attempt to disguise the cause of death.

However, young Mary Rogerson witnessed Ruxton's act of madness and he had to silence her forever. There was evidence of blunt force trauma on the skull and he may then also have cut her throat. This could have taken place on the stairway or landing and would have accounted for the heavy blood staining on the walls and carpets.

Having murdered two women, the doctor then used his medical knowledge to dispose of the bodies and, as we have seen, to remove identifying features. The bodies were manhandled into the bath and there he cut them up, limb from limb, piece by piece. The blood loss here would have been considerable and would have left heavy staining on the bath. He might also have cut his own hand by accident at this time. It would have taken about eight hours to complete but, once his bloody work was done, he kept the body parts in the two locked bedrooms until he was able to dispose of them. Had Mrs Hampshire managed to get into either of these rooms then she would have been in for a very nasty surprise.

And, all the while, his three children were sleeping in their own rooms, oblivious to the horrors that were taking place beyond their bedroom doors. In the end, it was local children who best summed up the events of that grim September night with a piece of doggerel:

> Red stains on the carpet, red stains on the knife,
> For Dr Buck Ruxton has murdered his wife.
> The maidservant saw it and threatened to tell,
> So Dr Buck Ruxton he's killed her as well.

There is a strange story of a visit made by Ruxton to a fortune teller who told him the number thirteen would play a distinctive role in his life – and it certainly did. He was arrested on 13 October, committed for trial on 13 December, sentenced to death on 13 March and his prison number was 8410 – which adds up to thirteen.

8

DEATH ON THE ROAD

James Robertson

At first it looked like a hit and run.

Taxi driver John Kennedy found the woman at just after midnight on 28 July 1950 lying on Glasgow's Prospecthill Road. He had just crested the brow of the steep hill that runs down towards the junction with Aikenhead Road on the city's south side when his headlights picked out the body. 'I thought perhaps she was drunk,' he said later, 'then I saw that her face was matted with blood.'

As he stooped over the woman, a Glasgow Corporation maintenance truck pulled up and the driver Samuel Murray and his pal David Ashe climbed out to help. They were part of a team repairing tram lines and had passed the same spot just ten minutes before and had noticed a dark coloured car sitting there with its lights off. Mr Ashe had said that, at the time, he thought he'd seen a woman lying on the road beside the car but Mr Murray was certain he had been mistaken. Clearly, though, there had been no mistake.

The alarm was raised and a police car was directed to the scene of what was still thought to be an accident. Constable William Kevan studied the area under the glare of various sets of headlights and torches. He was an experienced traffic cop and had attended many an accident. It did not take him long to realise that something did not add up here.

She had once been a good-looking woman but now her body

was battered and smashed. Her dark-red hair was matted with blood and blood was splattered all over her light-coloured coat. Her shattered dental plate was on the ground and her shoes lay some distance away. She was on her back with her arms slightly outstretched and one leg bent over the other. It was obvious she had been run over by a car. There were tyre marks around and on the body but, curiously, there was no other sign of the vehicle. We know now, from the plethora of forensic science documentaries and dramas, that it is virtually impossible for someone to enter or leave the scene of a crime without leaving or taking something that links them to it. Fingerprints are, of course, the most well-known things to be left behind but footprints, saliva, semen, hair, blood, traces of fabric can all be of help to police investigators. And, of course, now with DNA testing, the discovery of even a small amount of skin can be the equivalent of leaving behind your name and address.

A case of hit-and-run is no different from any other crime and Constable Kevan expected to find a piece of smashed headlamp or other pieces from the car but here there was nothing. Only the tyre marks in the road bore testimony to the presence of a vehicle. But, to his experienced eye, those tyre marks revealed a great deal. There were two sets of tracks, both showed signs of a car braking. Peering closely in the torchlight, he saw blood and bits of flesh between the treads and noted that the two streaks met beyond the body. On looking closer he was able to tell that the car had driven over the body more than once. In fact, he calculated that it had bumped over the poor woman no less than eight times, forward and back, forward and back, forward and back, forward and back.

Professor Andrew Allison, who had appeared in the Peter Queen case, and Dr James Innis carried out the post-mortem. Professor Allison later stated that the injuries were 'more gross than I have ever met with in an accident due to a private car'. PC Kevan felt that the woman had been knocked out somehow and placed in the road prior to the car being driven over her and the doctors agreed. They found a mark on her right temple that suggested she had been rendered unconscious by a blunt instrument. They also believed the injuries were not consistent with the woman being knocked down by a vehicle. Although the face, torso and pelvis were badly mangled by the wheels, the injuries to the legs were not what they would have expected if the woman had been hit by a speeding motor.

So, the medical evidence was that the woman had first been hit over the head with some form of club and then laid on the road before the killer drove the car over the body time and time again. It was an act of cold-blooded murder.

At 2.10 a.m. on the day the body was found, Constable 138D of the City of Glasgow Police force stood in the police box on Cumberland Street in the Gorbals and noted in the logbook:

> At 12.50 a.m. today a woman was knocked down and fatally injured in Prospecthill Road near Aikenhead Road. The motor car, believed to be a small, blue Austin, maybe 10hp, was driven by a man wearing a light-fawn Burberry coat. The car did not stop and was last seen driving eastwards on Aikenhead Road.

That police officer knew far more about the incident than those few lines would suggest. Unlike Constable Kevan, however, his knowledge did not come from deductive reasoning or even many years of experience. He knew because he had been there before anyone else.

He knew because he was the killer.

The dead woman was forty-year-old Catherine McCluskey, an unmarried mother of two who lived virtually on the breadline in Nicholson Street, in the Gorbals. When last seen alive, she had been dressed in her best clothes and was heading off to meet her boyfriend, leaving a friend to look after her children. When she did not return, her friend alerted the police after reading about the dead woman in Prospecthill Road.

Inquiries, naturally, focused on the identity of her gentleman friend and, within hours of the body being discovered, police had a strong lead. Catherine had told her friends that the man she was seeing was the father of her younger child and was, in fact, a police officer. Witnesses who had seen her in a dark Austin motor car with a man in police uniform confirmed this. Catherine had also told her girlfriends that the man was married but paid her an allowance of nine shillings a week for young John. But inquiries at the Public Assistance Office, the forerunner of the DSS, revealed that the woman had refused to identify her married lover by name. She had told them she was merely trying to obtain a weekly payment from him so that her unemployment benefit of 33 shillings (£1.65) per week or her supplementary benefit of eight shillings and sixpence (around 43 pence) would remain unaffected.

Then they hit pay dirt. Catherine had confided to one close friend that the officer's second name was Robertson and that he was stationed locally. Suspicion fell on James Robertson, based in the then Southern Division Headquarters in Oxford Street. He certainly looked the part of a ladykiller. A former aircraft engine inspector, six-feet-one James Ronald Robertson – Big Ronnie to his pals on the job – was a good-looking, well-built man. With his dark hair and neatly-trimmed pencil-thin moustache, he would not have looked out of place in a lounge suit, sipping cocktails and wooing ladies of uncertain age but of comfortable means. But Big Ronnie wasn't like that. He was a teetotaller and deeply religious, often attending meetings of the ultra-strict Plymouth Brethren. He was also married with two children. Looks aside, he was not the kind of man you would immediately associate with extra-marital flings, illegitimate children and murder most foul.

But Constable 138D James Robertson had been absent from his beat on the night of the murder. And of late he had been driving a dark Austin motor car.

In the eyes of Chief Inspector Donald 'Tiger' MacDougall, Big Ronnie was worthy of a tug.

Police officers generally work in pairs and Robertson's neighbour,

125

or partner, that night had been a PC Dugald Moffat, who told Chief Inspector MacDougall that they had left Oxford Street headquarters in Robertson's car to drive to their Gorbals beat. Robertson drove an Austin 16 and, at the briefing before they left to begin their nightshift, they had been told that such a car, registration number CVD 350, had been stolen from a city centre street in May and was still missing. Of course, no one thought that the car Robertson was driving was nicked. The registration was different – DYS 570 – and, anyway, he was a copper and coppers are above suspicion.

With the car parked in its usual spot in a lane near Cumberland Street, the two officers set out for their tour of duty. But, after quarter of an hour, Robertson told his partner that he wanted to leave the beat for a while. This was not an unusual request. Officers often attended to personal business during working hours and expected their neighbours to cover for them. Robertson had done this before and, when asked by PC Moffat what he was going to do, he stated, 'I'm taking a blonde home but I won't be as long as I was last night.' He then went off to retrieve his car, leaving his pal walking the streets alone.

Later, PC Moffat saw the light flashing on the top of the police box in Cumberland Street. At that time, the boxes were commonplace in the city streets but they have now vanished. In the days before personal radios, the police box was vital in keeping response times to crimes as swift as possible. Each box had a telephone and a logbook inside and, when the beat officers passed and saw the light flashing, they knew they were needed somewhere. The boxes were also handy for storing sandwiches, flasks of hot tea or soup and, on occasion, a nip of spirits to keep the cold nights at bay.

PC Moffat used his key to unlock the box and telephoned the station. There was a disturbance in Cavendish Street, he was told, and he and his neighbour were needed. But, at this point, Robertson was nowhere to be seen so PC Moffat attended the shout himself and, along with other officers, made a number of arrests. The prisoners were whisked off to Oxford Street for processing where Duty Sergeant MacAllister asked Moffat where PC Robertson was. The unwritten law of any police force is that you back up your fellow officers no matter what so PC Moffat told the sergeant he was in the toilet. However, when Robertson failed to show up, it was suggested that perhaps he'd gone back out on his own. PC Moffat went out to find him, accompanied by the no doubt suspicious Sergeant MacAllister. At just after one in the morning, a much-relieved Dugald Moffat saw his partner hurrying along the street towards him. The quick-thinking Robertson told the sceptical sergeant that he had been in the station all along but had missed them.

Robertson was not as dapper as normal. PC Moffat saw sweat marks on his collar and, when he took off his hat, dark, wet stains could be seen on the band. He could also see dirt on the man's shoes and trousers. When they were alone again, Robertson told his partner his exhaust had broken off in Cathcart Road and he must've roared down it sounding 'like a Spitfire'. He'd had to stop and tie it up to the handle of one of the doors with a piece of rope, which was why he had been away for so long. Robertson later told another policeman the same story. This officer believed that Robertson was merely looking after the car for a friend of his brother who was out of the country.

Tiger MacDougall learned all this before he went anywhere near Robertson. But, within a day of Catherine McCluskey being found dead in the road, he felt he had enough to confront him and so, at 1.45 a.m. on July 29, he and Duty Sergeant MacAllister cornered the murder suspect while he was walking the beat in Eglinton Street.

'Is there any need to tell you who this is?' asked Sergeant MacAllister.

'Oh, no,' replied Robertson, 'it's Mr MacDougall.' Tiger was a well-known face on the force – and he had, somewhat embarrassingly, been given a lift in Robertson's car on occasion. He told the man why he wanted to speak to him and delivered the formal caution. He told him he thought he had murdered Catherine McCluskey.

'That, sir,' said Robertson, 'is entirely wrong.' But the experienced detective was unconvinced by this and, after the initial interview, he had Robertson formally charged in the police station. Robertson, who knew how to play the game, said for the record, 'There is nothing more I can say. I have already replied to Mr MacDougall.'

Before being locked in a cell, Robertson was searched and a non-standard issue rubber baton was found in his pocket. Although it was not uncommon for officers to carry makeshift weapons for additional protection on the streets, they also knew Catherine McCluskey had been rendered unconscious by a blow to the temple with such a weapon – and there was a suspicious looking stain on this one. The truncheon was sent to the forensic boffins who tested the stain. However, the most they could say was that the mark was possibly blood but the sample was just not large enough to allow them to be more specific.

Robertson's car was also sent for analysis. The exhaust was damaged but it had not simply dropped off as Robertson had suggested. The considered scientific opinion was that it had struck a 'soft-bodied object' which had snapped the silencer from the chassis, forcing it upwards, where it wedged against the propeller shaft. The 'soft-bodied object', they believed, had then been bounced towards the rear wheel and had come out from under the vehicle from underneath the front wheel. Of course, the 'soft-bodied object', it was suggested, was none other than poor Catherine McCluskey. They found blood and what appeared to be hair on the underside of the car – although some of the hair was described as being only 'closely similar' to the deceased and the rest of it undoubtedly came from an animal, possibly a dog. However, fragments of human flesh were found clinging to the bottom of the car, as were fibres which matched the dead woman's clothes.

Professor John Glaister had now become involved in the scientific investigation. In the yard of Oxford Street police station, he recreated the crime using the car and a policewoman volunteer who was similar to Catherine McCluskey in weight and build. On studying the medical reports, he learned that the only injuries to the deceased's legs were on the inside of her knees and not on the front or back, as he would have expected in a road accident. His findings, along with the medical reports, proved that the woman had been lying down on the road, insensible, before the car had run over her up to eight times.

Meanwhile, officers had searched Robertson's home and, in a tallboy, they found two motor registration books and a key ring with eighteen different car keys. They also discovered a wireless set and a number of other registration books which, they later learned, had been stolen from a Cumberland Street garage on 23 April. When confronted in an interview room, Robertson said he'd found the radio and books in the backcourt of a tenement. When questioned about the car, he said he'd found it abandoned in Hillington Road. He claimed it had been sitting there for two days before he decided to take it. He admitted passing the car off as his own and changing the number plates, using the registration of an Ayrshire farmer's tractor. He was, after all, facing a capital murder charge and putting his hands up to the relatively minor offence of 'taking and driving away' would have seemed attractive.

However, things were still looking black for James Robertson who continued to deny all knowledge of Catherine McCluskey and how she had died. But, as the evidence mounted against him, he changed his story. He admitted that he and Catherine had been romantically linked but he had not killed her. His solicitor, Laurence Dowdall, and defence counsel, John Cameron KC, told him his only hope of avoiding the gallows was to be perfectly honest about his involvement with the dead woman. At first, Robertson agreed. But, like many another accused before and since, he thought he knew better than his advisors.

So the case was ready to go to court. It had all the ingredients to make it the most talked about trial of the year in Glasgow. There was sex, there was death and there was a killer cop. Naturally, the crowds wanted to be in on it all. Outside Glasgow's High Court on the Saltmarket, the queues began to form at 7.30 a.m. on Monday 6 November 1950. Across the road stood the site of the old public gallows where Dr Pritchard had breathed his last but it is unlikely that anyone thought about that as they waited on that chilly morning for the doors to open on the latest murder sensation. They waited patiently, many knowing they were unlikely to grab a space in the public gallery first time round but, so keen was the interest, they were willing to wait for someone to leave. Seasoned trial-attenders had come prepared with sandwiches, flasks and even blankets.

The entire affair had to be settled by Wednesday 16 November. This was because, at the time, one of the distinctive aspects of the Scottish Criminal Procedures Act was that a trial had to be concluded within 110 days of a person's arrest – which, in this case, had been 29 July. Nowadays, the rule has been relaxed so that the trial need only begin within the 110 days. In the end, though, the Robertson case would only last a week and, despite the strong prosecution case, based largely on the scientific evidence, things were looking pretty hopeful for the accused.

But then, unexpectedly, the Crown was handed its best witness. The Crown case was that he had removed a troublesome mistress who had threatened the security of his marriage. His defence team valiantly tilted at the prosecution windmill, trying hard to suggest an alternative to their assertion that their client had first battered Catherine McCluskey then repeatedly ran over her unconscious body with his car. They suggested that the woman could have been knocked down accidentally by the car reversing on the hill. But, in order for a jury to accept that possibility, they had to push their legal lance through the scientific evidence.

Professor Glaister and John Cameron faced each other across the courtroom and discussed the flesh that had been ripped from the woman's legs. The astute forensic scientist pointed out the wounds were not on the knees. 'They are on the inner aspects of the knees and my experience of the female anatomy is that a woman does not stand presenting that part to an oncoming car.'

However, there was a small bump found on the rear bumper of the car and the equally as astute KC asked, 'So far as the motor car is concerned, there is evidence on the rear which is at least consistent with collision between the car in reverse and a human body?'

'Among other things,' replied Professor Glaister.

But Mr Cameron was not to be put off. 'But it is at least consistent with a human body?'

For his part, Professor Glaister was not going to be drawn quite so easily. 'That is one of a vast collection that could not be eliminated.'

'You cannot eliminate it?'

'No.'

It was a telling exchange and went some way to raising doubts over the prosecution case. However, try as they might, the defence could not completely undermine the prosecution claim that Catherine had been knocked out first – although they did produce their own expert witness who testified that it was possible the death was accidental. Mr Cameron also showed, using Laurence Dowdall as an assistant, that it was nigh on impossible for a right-handed man to stun a car passenger while sitting in the driving seat. Also, they had managed to cast doubts on at least some of the identification evidence, which is often the weakest part of any prosecution case. In this trial, although witnesses had picked out the accused at identification parades, one failed to recognise him in court and pointed instead to a journalist in the press box. Such court testimony is usually laughable at the best of times as the accused is generally the only one sitting between two big police officers. In this case, that particular piece of testimony reached the level of farce.

By the fifth day, the defence felt they had done a good enough job to at least merit a guilty verdict on a lesser charge and save their client from the hangman's tender mercies. But then the Crown was handed its star witness – James Robertson himself. He had been advised to come clean about his affair with the dead woman but, on the eve of taking the stand, he decided he could not embarrass his family. Laurence Dowdall and John Cameron tried to talk him out of this suicidal course of action but he was adamant. They had done a terrific job on his part and he was confident he would not be found guilty of murder. The jury would believe him.

In court, he said he had met Catherine McCluskey while on duty and attending a disturbance in Nicholson Street. After that, his acquaintanceship with her was merely a passing one – although he had once given the woman and her children a run home but had not gone inside.

On the night she died, Catherine McCluskey had asked to meet him. She had been unable to pay her rent and was threatened with eviction. She wanted him to drive her to a friend in Neilston, between Glasgow and Paisley, to see if she could arrange digs. He had told her he was working and could not drive her all the way to Neilston and, at that, she began to cry. While he was trying to calm her down, he drove her along Pollokshaws Road and Cathcart Road, finally reaching the hill on Prospecthill Road, where he stopped. She asked him to take her to Rutherglen but again he refused. He turned the car until it was facing back the way they had come. He told her he was going back to his beat and, if she was going, then she should go because he was not waiting there any longer. He opened the car door and she got out.

The court stilled as he spoke in a soft voice, giving his version of what happened next. 'I told her I was going back to Cumberland Street but, if she insisted on standing there, she would be left. At that time, the car door was open. I shut the door. She was standing on the pavement on the south side of the road.' He said he had started the car again and left her there but, after driving for about 100 yards, he thought better of it and decided to go back for her. 'It was very dark and there are no street lamps there. I reversed back to where I thought she was. I was on the crown of the road most of the time and gradually steered the car back to the pavement.' That was when he must have hit her. He noticed the tone of the engine changing and a 'bit of a jar'. He looked around in the darkness but could not see the woman anywhere. Then he opened the offside front door and began to get out.

'I saw her face on the ground below the offside running board, immediately beside the offside front tyre. I knelt down. It was Catherine McCluskey.' Her face was slightly to one side and he turned it over. Blood bubbled from her mouth then receded again. He looked under the car and saw that she had been caught up on the propeller shaft. He reached under to free her but she was well and truly stuck. He also knew she was well and truly dead. And then the gravity of his situation dawned on him. He was a serving police officer, away from his beat, driving a stolen car with a dead woman on his hands. Panic set in. Switching off the headlamps, he considered jacking the car up to free her but was unsure if he would be able to raise it far enough. Then he thought he might be able to dislodge the body by driving forward a bit. This did not work, so he reversed again – still no luck. He tried the manoeuvre again and this time he felt the body jerk free. Still in a state of fright, he drove off, leaving the mangled woman lying in the roadway behind him. At some point, probably in Cathcart Road as he had told PC Moffat, he became aware of the roaring of the engine and he stopped to tie up the damaged exhaust.

John Cameron looked at his client in the face and asked, 'On July 28 1950, did you assault Catherine McCluskey?'

James Robertson stared back at him and stated firmly, 'I did not.'

'Did you strike her on the head with a rubber truncheon?'

'No, sir.'

'Did you do anything to render her unconscious?'

'No, sir.'

'Did you deliberately drive a motor car over her and murder her?'

'No, sir, I did not.'

Harold Leslie KC, prosecuting, accused, 'Is it not the case that, before you got that woman out of the car, you struck her with a rubber truncheon?'

'No, certainly that is not the case,' Robertson replied, his voice by now little more than a whisper. 'I reversed the car into Catherine McCluskey and killed her but it was an accident.'

Robertson had been confident that the jury would believe his story but that confidence was misplaced. They were out for just one hour and three minutes and, when they returned, they found him unanimously guilty of stealing the car and the logbooks and guilty by a majority of murder. As the foreman read the verdict, Robertson, who had until then kept his gaze firmly on a spot just below the bench, turned and stared coldly at the eight men and seven women. He saw the fifteen faces that had considered his case, saw some of the women crying and saw that his gamble had failed.

There was only one sentence for murder and the judge settled the black cap on his head and pronounced it for doom. As Robertson was led away, word of the verdict was carried from mouth to mouth to the crowds outside. The people jostled and pushed to catch a glimpse of the convicted killer as he was hustled into the waiting van to take him to Barlinnie Prison, the Big House on the Hill, but his former colleagues on the force had erected a tarpaulin to block their view. As the van turned on to the Saltmarket, the sea of jeering and cheering people parted to allow it to turn towards High Street.

An appeal was lodged and duly denied. A plea for clemency was made and duly refused. On 16 December 1950, a noticeably thinner and hollow-eyed James Robertson was taken from the condemned cell to the specially prepared gallows room in the Big House where he paid the ultimate penalty.

To the end, his wife refused to believe her husband was a killer. The very thought was 'absolutely ridiculous'. She told a reporter, 'The facts are that my husband never went out by himself. He was keen on his hobbies, gardening and carpentry, and when he went out he took us all with him and, at times, the children only.'

But the facts were that James Robertson *had* been seeing Catherine McCluskey and had, in all probability, killed her – whether accidentally or with malice aforethought. As his own solicitor, Laurence Dowdall, said later, he was 'the fellow who chose to hang rather than let his wife down in public'.

9

THE LOVE THAT DARE NOT SPEAK ITS NAME

Robert Scott

It was civilian plumber William Young's habit to lock the prisoner in the workshop while he went for his tea break. The lad had been working with him for a year, had proved a trustworthy and willing assistant and, while Mr Young was away for his morning cuppa, had simply continued in his labours.

But this time it was different. This time the young man had something on his mind. And, as he heard the plumber turning the key in the door lock, whatever it was that was preying on him took hold.

Perhaps he sat for a few minutes and thought about what he was going to do. Perhaps he thought about the events that had led him to this point in his young life. Perhaps, as the final seconds of that life ticked by, he thought back five years, to a different time and a different place when he was a very different person . . .

Robert Scott first met William Vincent at a car coffee bar near the Graham Square Car Market in the east end of Glasgow early in 1954. They had little in common. Robert was a seventeen-year-old, handsome, muscular east-ender from Forge Street in Parkhead; William was older, bespectacled but dapper and owned his own business in the city's trendy west end. He made a bit of money on the side as a police informer but that did not come out until after his death. He was also a homosexual with a taste for good-looking

136

young men – and the well-built Robert Scott fitted that bill perfectly. But, on their first meeting, all they did was talk, for, at that stage, the younger man's dreams were leading him elsewhere. They were common, everyday dreams for most young people – of fame, perhaps, of fortune, definitely. His dreams took him from that coffee bar and from the east end that was his home to the bright lights of London, where the streets are paved with gold. But, within weeks, he realised that those bright lights hid a dark side and the pavements were not gilded but hard and cold and grey.

Four months later, in the summer of 1954, he was back in his home town and at another coffee stall, this time in St Vincent Street, he bumped into William Vincent again. It's possible Robert knew William was homosexual. It's possible he knew he was being chatted up. It's possible he had his own leanings in that direction. However, it's equally as possible he didn't know any of these things, believing the man's interest was merely friendly. Whatever the truth, he refused William's offer of another coffee, saying he had to dash for a bus. Vincent told him he had his car nearby and offered to run him home. Robert, though, refused – although he did agree to meet the man the following Saturday for a drink.

They met in a pub in the city centre and then moved on to the Crocodile Club in Park Circus. William was a generous host. He kept getting them in and Robert kept knocking them back until he was as drunk as the proverbial lord.

Finally, as the night grew old, the young man thought of wending his weary way home across the city. But William would not hear of it. He only lived round the corner, he said. There was no need to go all the way to Parkhead, he said and invited him to stay the night at his mews flat at 43 Park Terrace Lane, above his thriving car spraying business. At one time, they had been coachman's apartments and stables respectively but that was in the days of yore and the horseless carriage had put paid to all that. There was, however, still an air of Victorian charm about the lane, with its cobblestones and gas-powered street lighting. It is doubtful, though, if the somewhat worse for drink Robert Scott appreciated its olde worlde appeal on his first visit. He spent the night in William's bed, too drunk, he said later, to recall what, if anything, happened.

As it turned out, it was the beginning of what would become a far from beautiful friendship. At first, everything seemed fine. William seemed to be passionately in love with his young friend – or at least hopelessly obsessed with him – and Robert was sufficiently happy with the relationship to take him home to meet the parents. Bill, as he was introduced, launched an immediate charm offensive. He took them for trips in his gleaming Jaguar. He invited them to tea in his tastefully decorated flat. He said he had big plans for Bob. He would set him up in business, perhaps even make him a partner in his own firm.

But Bob's father, also called William, found something about the man's charm distinctly offensive. Although pleased that a new world of possibilities was opening up for his son, he did not fully trust this older man. Whether he suspected there was something more than friendship between the two men is unknown. Perhaps the thought never occurred to him. This was Britain in the 1950s and such things were not even thought of, let alone talked of, in most homes – and certainly not in the East End of Glasgow. The Friends of Dorothy had not yet appropriated the word gay and homosexual acts were still illegal. The idea of his son having sex with another man might well have been the furthest thing from his mind.

And there is no evidence that there was anything physical between Bill and Bob at this stage. William Vincent was besotted by the younger man, of that there is no question, but there was the night when young Robert stormed angrily from the room when Bill and his friends were passing around photographs of naked young men. And, on another night, the young man rebuffed a sexual overture from Bill saying, 'Don't think I am like those other pals that you know.'

Robert Scott may well have been a homosexual who had been conditioned by society into convincing himself he was not. William

Vincent, later painted as a corrupting influence, may well have been a man aware of his own sexuality who recognised similar traits in a younger man. If he had been an older man who was pulling a younger woman, some might have regarded him as a dirty old man – others, of course, would have classed him as a lucky dirty old man. Heads would shake, tongues would cluck but he would have been accepted not reviled. As it was, especially after his death, he was painted as a pervert who preyed on the innocent. And that may actually have been the case.

Whatever the truth of their relationship, Robert Scott changed. His father said that he transformed from being happy to moody and unstable. It is possible he had become disenchanted with his friendship, realising he had drifted into a circle of which he wanted no part. It is also possible that he was battling his own urges – that he was, in fact, homosexual and his inability to accept it was having an effect on his psyche. It is known that he shared William's bed on more than one occasion. Society – not to mention the law – told him that such things were wrong and that would have brought him into conflict with his hormones. Whatever the case, forces were building inside him.

And, sooner or later, those forces would explode.

Perhaps he thought of these things as he sat in the workshop. Outside the locked door he would have heard the sounds of other prisoners going about their daily routine. A voice here, a whistle there, the clatter of work tools and buckets and other lives and other problems. But they were out there and he was in here and neither the twain would meet.

His gaffer had only been gone a few minutes but would be back soon.

He did not have much time . . .

Britain, in the 1950s, still called up its young men for National Service in the military. The scheme had been instituted in 1939 and continued until 1960, by which time over five million men had

139

gone through their period of service. In 1955, Robert Scott, drowning in a sea of self-recrimination and self-loathing, was thrown a lifeline. His call-up papers came through and he was posted to 16 Company, RAOC, at Longtown in Cumberland. The posting would get him away from William Vincent – away from the life into which he had somehow fallen. But Bill would not or could not forget his young love. He wrote to him constantly, telling him how much he missed him, how much he wished they were together again, kisses carefully crossed at the end of each loving note. In June 1957, Bill travelled south to Cumberland to meet up with the young squaddie in a hotel. He invited him up to his room while he changed and, once there, suddenly jumped on Robert and kissed him on the mouth. The young man jerked away feeling, he said later, 'terrible and disgusted'. William Vincent would try that trick once too often.

Robert Scott wanted to use his period of service to distance himself from the older man and his lifestyle. As time wore on, he stopped replying to Bill's letters. So Bill began to write to Bob's commanding officer asking if he knew why his young friend did not write back and requesting information about buying him out of the service. Although he was still fixated on Bob, he still had an eye for a cute young man. In 1957, he chatted up a Dundee youth in a Glasgow pub and took him home. Afterwards, he gave him a job but, within two weeks, his new-found love turned nasty, attacking him with a piece of rubber hose and leaving him bound and gagged and light of a ring, a watch and over £100 in cash. A desperate letter was dashed off to the Cumberland CO asking if Robert could be given special leave but the young man refused to come home.

In January 1958, Robert received his discharge papers and headed back to Glasgow. William was at the station to greet him but his joy soon turned to despair and then anger when the young man told him he wanted to go home to see his parents. Robert had grown up during his stint in the army and he wanted nothing more to do with William Vincent. He returned the gold cigarette case that Vincent had given him. He told him he never wanted to talk to him again. He was not to phone and he was not to write. Whatever there had been between them before was now over.

But the phone calls and the letters and the pleas to meet kept coming. Furious at his rejection, William threatened to tell the young man's parents exactly what he got up to on those many nights he stayed in the west end flat. A meeting was actually arranged between William Vincent and the Scott family but it degenerated into an argument and things were said on both sides that everyone would live to regret. Robert Scott stormed from the room, vowing never to talk to any one of them again.

From that moment he tried to make it on his own. He moved in with a friend. He found a job as a salesman and even worked nights as a waiter in a New City Road bar. But William Vincent was always in the background, asking him to come back, begging him to return, pleading for one more chance. Finally, Robert wanted to finish it once and for all. He decided to meet up with the older man and tell him that there was no hope for them, now or ever. On Saturday 12 April, after he finished work in the bar, he went to a late-night club where he thought he would find Bill. But the man was not there that night so Robert, desperate to see things through, phoned him at home. Bill told him that, if he wanted to see him, he should come round to the flat. It was nearing midnight but Robert agreed to go. He wanted things to end that night. He wanted to be free.

He had the rope in his hands now He had wanted things to end that night in 1958 and they had but not the way he'd planned. Now they would finally end. Now he would put a stop to the despair and the anguish and the pain.

It is just a simple thing. Stand on the metal work table, throw it over the beam, loop it round his neck and step off. It would be all over soon.

He would be free.

Robert Scott walked through the night to Park Terrace Lane, his coat hunched around him to keep out the cold. He had no idea what was going to happen. He thought he was going to finish a chapter of his life that would, as far as he was concerned, have been better not written. In reality, he was going to destroy two lives.

And what were William Vincent's intentions that night? Probably what they always were – to win Robert's affections once more. He had never given up hope that the two of them could be together again. Sure, he had been far from faithful but what was he, a monk? He had needs and, if Robert would not fulfil them, then he needed to find others who would. But that did not mean he did not love the lad. Or perhaps William Vincent was simply that most pathetic of creatures – a possessive, obsessive older man infatuated with an attractive younger person he could not have.

Whatever his motivations, he made his final, fatal error as soon as he let Robert in. He did what he always did – he threw himself at the young man and tried to kiss him. On previous occasions, Robert had simply pulled back from such embraces but this time something inside snapped. This time he wanted to show Bill just how revolted and disgusted and so utterly sick he was of the whole affair. This time he would end it all forever and completely.

He did not mean to kill William Vincent. He just wanted the man to see how serious he was. He just wanted to hold him against the wall, his fingers clamped round his throat, to show him that he meant it when he said it was over. He just wanted Bill to realise that it all had to stop.

It wasn't until Bill's eyes fluttered and his struggles weakened and his body was hanging limp in his grasp that Robert realised he'd gone too far. He loosened his grip and saw that his fingers had dug into the flesh around the man's throat, drawing blood. He let the body slip carefully to the floor and felt for a pulse and a heartbeat but nothing pounded at his wrist or throbbed in his chest. William Vincent was dead.

Then Robert did something strange. He took one of the man's

socks off and placed it at his neck to staunch the blood flow from the wounds. Exactly why he did this is unclear.

His thoughts then turned, as thoughts often do in desperate situations, to flight. He did not have murder in mind when he set out that night but plenty of men had been hanged who did not set out to kill. He needed to get rid of the body and he needed to get away. It is not known exactly at what point he decided to return to Cumberland, where he had been stationed – where he had been happy – but that's where he ended up. He had dragged the corpse out of the flat and bundled it into the boot of William's own 1956 yellow and red Sunbeam Talbot Alpine. He drove the ninety miles south in a daze, finally reaching Blackbank Wood near his old base in Longtown. He thought he could hide the body here, then return home. With any luck, the corpse would never be discovered and he would be able to live his life the way he wanted. He turned on to a woodland track to seek out a likely spot for a makeshift burial.

Maybe he knew the game was up when the car's wheels became bogged down in thick mud. He possibly knew when he walked to the army base guardhouse and asked for help to free his car from the ditch. He certainly knew, after being told there was no help available, when he asked to use the phone and was connected to the police office at Gretna.

'I have done a murder,' he said. 'If you come to the 16th Company guardroom I will show you a body.'

A policeman arrived from Longtown and Robert took him to where the brightly coloured car was stuck in the mud. He opened the boot and stepped back to let the police officer see inside. William Vincent was curled up inside, his knees to his chest, wearing only a shirt, trousers and one sock. The other sock was still wrapped round the wounds on his neck.

As the forensic teams arrived with their cameras and their tape measures and their evidence bags, Robert Scott was taken away by CID to Longtown. 'I have saved some people a lot of misery,' he told officers.

Back in Glasgow, police officers forced their way into the flat and found bloodstains in the hallway and the mark in the dust of garage floor where Robert had hauled the body by the legs towards the car. Neighbours were questioned about the bachelor who lived nearby and details of his private life also began to be unearthed. Meanwhile, Glasgow police picked the suspect up from Cumberland and brought him back to Scotland to face trial. He travelled in a police car surrounded by officers while another copper followed in Bill's Sunbeam.

Robert Scott was formally charged in Partick Police Station – where Peter Queen had announced his wife's death a quarter century before – at 1.18 p.m. on Monday 14 April 1958. 'He tried to ruin my life and make me the same as him,' he said.

His parents, who had been enjoying an anniversary dinner on the night their son was committing murder, were informed the following day. William Scott visited his son on Tuesday. But the young man was ashamed of himself and refused to talk. His father, desperate for some form of communication, asked him if he had enough cigarettes. 'Yes, plenty,' said his son, turning away. 'Just leave me alone.'

There was little sympathy shown for the victim at the trial in July. Even the trial judge, Lord Russell, called him a 'worthless man' but did warn the jury that this was 'not a court of morals but a court of law' and they had to put their 'personal revulsion' aside when deciding Robert Scott's fate. He also reminded them that no one had the right to set himself up as an executioner, no matter how 'worthless' the victim.

It took the ten men and five women only thirty-two minutes to decide that Robert Scott was guilty of murder. At the time, hanging was still the ultimate penalty for murder but Scottish courts had some distaste for the sentence and, anyway, there was sympathy for the young man in the light green jacket in the dock. He was sentenced to life imprisonment with no minimum period set.

He began his new life as a convict in Perth Prison and seemed to be doing well – until that Thursday in November 1959 when he tied a noose and completed the job the courts would not. Plumber

William Young returned after eight minutes to find him dangling from the roof beam. Why he felt the need to kill himself is a mystery. His letters home had been upbeat, hopeful that he could be freed soon pending a review of his case. He had been doing well in prison, had no complaints, no obvious problems. But something was obviously wrong – and his father, speaking after his son's death, knew where to lay the blame. William Vincent had somehow reached out from beyond the grave and had hurt his son for the last time.

'That loathsome creature and the other corrupters who surrounded him,' he said, 'they are the men responsible for his death.'

Robert Scott was only twenty-two years of age.

10

POISONED RELATIONSHIPS

1. Anne Marie Lindsay

Peter Lindsay began to feel ill after he'd eaten the stew. At first he thought there had simply been too much rosemary in the sauce – he told his wife there should only be a pinch or two – but, when he began to vomit, he suspected he had a touch of gastro-enteritis. He went to the doctor the following day and was given some pills to help ease his stomach. But no pills would ease what ailed him. Two weeks later he was dead – and, in a dying deposition, he implicated his young wife as the person who put the lethal weedkiller in his food.

Anne Marie Farrell was born in London in 1952 but moved to Australia with her family when she was just over two years of age. She met Scotsman Peter Lindsay when she was around twelve. He had left his family farm at Foulden Hill near Aytoun in Berwickshire at the age of nineteen in 1964 to make his own way in Australia. By the time she was sixteen, he had become something more than a friend – in fact, she was pregnant by him. In 1968, they were married in Adelaide and, soon after, their first child, a boy, was born. Another child, a daughter, would be born three years later.

But things did not go smoothly for the young newly-weds. Anne Marie was still little more than a child herself and was unhappy with the life of a wife and mother. Her friends were all

146

out enjoying themselves and she was stuck at home looking after her husband and the children. She was an attractive, intelligent and charming young woman. She was also, according to one person, very shrewd. But none of these attributes prevented the onset of clinical depression and its demon familiar – thoughts of suicide. Medical help was sought and the young woman had to be admitted to Hillcrest Mental Hospital in Adelaide for treatment. She also found solace outside her marriage, embarking on an affair with an older married man with three children of his own.

In 1973, Peter returned home to Scotland to take his place in the family farming business. The idea was that Anne Marie would join him as soon as she was well enough. Medical clearance came for her to leave the country only half an hour before her flight was due to take off for Heathrow.

If the move back to Scotland was meant to change things, it is difficult to see how. Anne Marie was desperately unhappy in Australia but at least there she had her family and friends around her. It was unlikely that a move to border farming in Scotland would be an improvement. There was very little for a young smart girl who wanted to enjoy life to do. Her husband played cricket in the village of Manderston, for a team captained by his brother, and he would take her to the cricket club on a Sunday evening but this was hardly the high life. Anne Marie herself was reported as describing the nights out as 'not exactly exciting'.

Naturally, then, the move to Scotland did not improve their relationship. Their sexual life broke down completely because, it was later said, they did not want to have any more children. The contraceptive pill did not agree with her and although she'd had a coil fitted it would not stay in place. She also admitted in an essay about herself, sent to Peter's sister, that 'although I try I cannot get emotionally involved in anything I do, or in the people I meet . . . I think this explains my attitude to sex. Although I enjoy it, afterwards I feel wanton and disgusted with myself. It is an involuntary psychological block.' She also stated that she loved her children but added, 'yet [I] hate them because they tie me to a life I hate. Why should I lock myself away in a house in a strange country I don't like?' She also said, 'At times I believe I am not actually human and that is not good for anyone.' She went on to describe herself in this curious essay as 'selfish, hard-hearted and mercenary'. These words would come back to haunt her in the courtroom.

Other letters were found in the farmhouse following her husband's death. One was to a man named Joe in Australia in which she stated, 'I have a plan up my sleeve but I can't tell you anything about it.' Joe was someone she had known in Adelaide but Peter had found out about him 'thanks to [his] big sister'. The letter made it clear he was coming over to Scotland and she was delighted with the prospect but was unsure how her husband would react.

She also sent letters to another man in Australia named Stephen, for whom she had 'strong feelings'. In one, she said, 'I can't live without you but I can't live without [my children].' But Stephen was a homosexual and they had met while she was in the mental hospital. She was very fond of him as she was of Joe, who was just another friend. The plan she had mentioned in her letter was merely about a holiday.

The hospital may well have thought she was well enough to move to Scotland but clearly she was not. The depression returned very soon after she arrived at the border farm. She again threatened to take her own life, once, in January 1974, even getting the length of taking an overdose of tablets. She was rushed to Berwick Infirmary but later transferred to a psychiatric hospital for treatment. But her mental state did not improve and when she suggested to Peter that she take the children back to Australia, he refused. But she wanted her life back. She wanted to be young and carefree. She wanted her independence.

According to the prosecution, she made her big bid for that independence, fittingly, on July 4, 1974. She cooked her husband a casserole of stewing steak, onions and sauce consisting of tomatoes, vinegar and a pinch of rosemary. But there was another, secret ingredient – Gramoxone, a paraquat weedkiller.

Paraquat had been much in the news that year. Children had been poisoned accidentally by the deadly substance and the newspapers had been filled with reports of a case in England where a twenty-two-year-old housewife had murdered her husband by lacing a stew with the stuff.

Peter Lindsay knew he had some Gramoxone on the farm. It was kept in a gallon container although there was only a cupful left. What he did not expect to discover was that some of it had made its way into his evening meal. But it had.

Later, as he lay dying in Edinburgh Royal Infirmary, he gave a statement to a sheriff. He said he had detected a strange taste in his meal and commented on it to his wife, telling her she had put too much rosemary in the sauce. Then he 'felt queasy' and began to be violently ill. He said he thought at first it was a touch of gastro but, when it continued the following morning, he attended the doctor. Within two weeks he was dead. His mother said that, shortly before he died, he told her, 'What a stupid little wife to try to murder me.'

One expert said that half a tablespoon of paraquat would be enough to kill a person. It was thought he'd had up to nine spoonfuls. His mouth, throat and lungs had been badly burned by the poison, which was known to corrode mild steel. The liver and kidneys were severely damaged. Just how the lethal substance had got into the stew was the thing that had to be established. Naturally, Anne Marie was asked this and, at first, she said their daughter had brought the container into the house. She took it off the child and poured the contents down the sink, near where she was preparing the stew. It was possible some of it had splashed onto the food, she suggested. Later she changed that statement, saying that she had brought to container into the house herself. But she insisted that the poison had made its way into the food accidentally. But the experts were having none of that. Tests had shown that it was impossible to pour as much as nine tablespoons of Gramoxone accidentally on to the food.

Also, a doctor spoke of Anne Marie's reaction to the news that her husband had been poisoned by paraquat. 'I don't think I have ever seen such a lack of reaction to such serious news in thirty-seven years of practice,' said Dr Henry Matthews of the Scottish Poisons Bureau. But Anne Marie insisted her husband's death was accidental. Facing trial in the High Court at Jedburgh in January 1975, she said, 'The fact that his death was accidental has made no difference to the way I feel about the matter. I can't honestly see how I could live with the knowledge that his death was my fault . . . I can never clear my mind of what happened. I seem to have lost track of what actually happened.'

But the prosecution was quite clear about what they thought happened. She wanted rid of her husband, they claimed. There was the financial attraction of several thousand pounds' worth of insurance policies – and there was the prospect of freeing herself from an unhappy marriage.

But the defence insisted it was accidental. In the witness box for five hours, the accused was asked pointedly, 'Did you intentionally poison your husband?'

Looking directly at the jurors, she replied, 'I did not. I swear before God, I did not.' But it did not save her. At the end of the four-day trial, the jury took sixty-three minutes to return a majority verdict of guilty. As the judge sentenced her to life in prison, Anne Marie Lindsay, still only twenty-four, swayed in the dock and collapsed, striking her head against the rail. Two police officers carried her to the cells below to begin her new life.

Twenty years later, another marriage would be ripped apart by poison. Luckily, no one died as a result – but it wasn't for want of trying.

2. Dr Paul Agutter

It was an extortion plot involving paraquat that might have set the murder plan in motion.

In 1987, a mysterious figure using the pen name The Raven set out to systematically wring cash from the Edinburgh outlets of supermarket giants Safeway. He – or she, for the culprit was never caught – came, figuratively, tapping at their chamber door to tell them coleslaw jars and grapefruit juice had been laced with either the weedkiller or ground glass. Thoughtfully warning labels were left on the packaging. If the company paid up, The Raven would stop. If not, then the campaign would continue and perhaps next time there would be no warning posted. In other words, Safeway either coughed up – or some customers would cough their last. Surely it was worth £100,000 to protect their business? In the end, the company did not pay up and The Raven flew away, nameless forever more.

Learning their lesson, Safeway invested in close circuit TV cameras in their properties. And it was this technology that would prove the downfall of the next would-be poisoner to use their shelves as a means of retailing murder.

In late August 1994, Edinburgh was buzzing with its annual Festival fever. On stages all over the city drama groups were presenting shows that ranged from the run-of-the-mill to the wild and wacky. But, at the same time, in the city, there was a real-life drama being enacted that would made many fictional murder stories seem humdrum. The Safeway store at Hunter's Tryst, in Edinburgh, sold, as it normally does, a number of bottles of tonic water. One of the customers was Elizabeth Sharwood-Smith and she bought a two-litre bottle and took it home. She and her husband were expecting friends from England. They were all going to see a play at the Festival and they would appreciate a nice gin and tonic after their long journey.

On Wednesday 24 August, Mrs Sharwood-Smith decided to have a pre-dinner drink, so she poured herself a vermouth and tonic and her eldest son, Andrew, sipped a glass of straight tonic. They became ill almost immediately. Their mouths dried. They hallucinated. Their pulses raced, reaching 140 beats per minute. They experienced temporary blindness. But, despite all that, they were very lucky – very lucky indeed. They survived.

Geoffrey Sharwood-Smith, a consultant anaesthetist at Edinburgh Royal Infirmary, suspected some form of poisoning. His suspicions were supported by his houseguests who just happened to be a chemist, with an interest in hallucinogens and their effects, and her neuropathologist husband. But, if the Sharwood-Smiths had been poisoned accidentally, what was the source? The symptoms suggested poisoning by atropine, which is derived from nightshade berries, so the garden was searched, just in case some had been picked by mistake. But no such berries were found and it looked like the source of the poisoning would remain a mystery. At this stage, no one thought to investigate the tonic water. Luckily, the guests never did have their gin and tonic and made do with a cup of tea instead. As Dr Sharwood-Smith later recalled, one of the guests had said she could have killed a gin and tonic 'but two large ones would have killed her'.

By the Friday, both Mrs Sharwood-Smith and her son had recovered but their new found health would not last long. For, later that night, they drank more of the tonic water and, this time, the woman was stricken with paralysis and her son was, once again, hallucinating. If left untreated, they would have slipped into a coma and died of heart or respiratory failure. Dr Sharwood-Smith went with his wife and son in the ambulance and, by now convinced they had been poisoned, managed to gather enough information to identify the tonic water as the source. At the hospital, though, his claims that his wife and son had been poisoned by atropine in a bottle of tonic water, plucked at random from the shelves of a large supermarket, were met with disbelief. However, the medical team treated the patients who, once again, cheated death.

The following day, Dr Sharwood-Smith went to the Hunter's Tryst Safeway and convinced the manager to take all the bottles of tonic water from the shelves. He also took a sample from his own bottle for analysis. But there was still a feeling of disbelief over everything – until the Sunday when two more cases of suspected atropine poisoning were rushed into the Infirmary. Eventually, a total of eight people suffered the effects.

Analysis revealed that the bottle bought by Mrs Sharwood-Smith contained enough atropine to kill fifteen people. Now it was certain. The atropine had to have been placed in the tonic water purposely – there was no other explanation. Fears that The Raven had flown back in fluttered in the corporate mind. Was he back to his old tricks again? If so, there was no warning, no extortion attempt. Whoever had placed the deadly poison in the tonic water had done so deliberately and with malice aforethought. This was meant to kill. But who would do such a thing? And why?

One of the Sunday victims was a thirty-nine-year-old woman named Alexandra Agutter and, with the hospital alerting the police that there was a possible mass poisoner on the loose, the first step for detectives was to talk to the families. Her husband, forty-eight-year-old Paul Agutter was a lecturer in biochemistry at Edinburgh's Napier University. He was, of course, distraught that his wife had had such a close brush with death. They had been in their home at Athelstaneford, East Lothian, that Sunday night when she had asked him for a gin and tonic. He poured it for her, declining to take one himself because he had to drive the gardener home. Naturally, he had no idea that the tonic was poisoned. He had contacted his GP by phone when she became ill but only managed to reach an answering service. Luckily for Mrs Agutter, though, a locum picked up the message very quickly and came right round to the house. An ambulanceman from the Royal Infirmary took the remains of the drink away for examination.

Safeway moved quickly to eliminate any possibility of further poisonings. They had their drink shelves cleared by early Monday morning, not just in Edinburgh but across the country, and public appeals were made, with Dr Sharwood-Smith himself explaining the dangers of atropine. He described the poisonings as 'the work of an evil and twisted mind'. It was also pointed out that, if someone of frail health or suffering from a heart condition had drunk the tonic, they would have had a death on their hands. Dr Agutter also spoke to the press, saying, 'It is beyond me to imagine what type of person would do this.' Later, he told detectives, 'To tell you the truth, if I got hold of the blighter, I would kill him on the spot.'

Within hours of the appeals, the police had received over 100 calls from a worried public.

Bonded by their mutual victimisation at the hands of some deranged mass poisoner, Dr Agutter made contact with the Sharwood-Smiths, talking to them about atropine and showing off quite considerable knowledge of its lethal properties. 'He knew how much you could put in before you could taste it because it would have a bitter taste,' said Elizabeth Sharwood-Smith at the trial.

'I was astonished by this,' said her husband later in the *Glasgow Herald*. 'Even though he was a biochemist it was an odd thing to know.'

Police mounted a painstaking investigation to catch the poisoner before someone died. Safeway staff members were interviewed to see if any of them had a beef with their employers but they were all cleared. One early theory that an ex-serviceman back from the first Gulf War with supplies of atropine and bearing some sort of grudge against society was also dropped. Then what appeared to be a strong lead turned up. A man who had earlier threatened to lace bottles of Lucozade with weedkiller and place them in shops used by Edinburgh police officers claimed responsibility for the atropine poisonings. Although the suspect was traced to a house not far from the Hunter's Tryst supermarket, it was subsequently found that he was not the culprit. He was charged with causing a public mischief and sent for psychiatric treatment.

But the public appeals were bringing results. More bottles were being returned and, more importantly, a part-time worker at the supermarket recalled seeing a man acting very suspiciously on Wednesday. At the time, the man was wearing a green coat and appeared to have bottles hidden underneath it. This was just five hours before Elizabeth Sharwood-Smith bought her bottle of tonic.

It was at this point that the security cameras, installed after The Raven's extortion attempt, proved their worth. Police had viewed them earlier but, armed with the worker's description, took a fresh look. This time they saw him – a man wearing a coat and a purple top. And he looked familiar.

Dr Paul Agutter was arrested at his home. Officers searching the house found the coat and the top he had worn the previous week. They also found a Safeway carrier bag and a till receipt for Wednesday 24 August.

The Agutters seemed to have what could be called an open marriage. In other words, they lived together but apparently enjoyed affairs with each other's knowledge. English-born Paul Agutter had been married before but, after five stormy years, it had collapsed. He married fellow academic Alexandra in 1976 and, with his degrees in molecular biology, became a lecturer in what was then Napier College. By 1994, the college had become a university and he had become a reader in cell biology. He was well liked by the students and many of his colleagues. He was, however, disliked by some for being too enthusiastic about his work.

At one point, Agutter listed his dislikes as 'pop music, television, nuclear power plants, badly-behaved dogs, idleness, Hirondelle red, psychiatrists and bureaucrats'. His likes included 'music, literature, open countryside, well-behaved dogs, Burgundy of respectable age, log fires and [his] work'.

He also had a yen to be a literary giant but, apart from scientific papers and one short story, he had not had much luck in print. His likes and dislikes were included in a biographical breakdown he provided with the manuscript of a novel he had written. The novel was rejected, at one point with the criticism that, although Agutter was 'not without talent', he had got carried away with his own ingenuity. It was that imagination and ingenuity that led him to devise his murder plan.

He had apparently fallen in love with another woman, a former student, and he wanted to spend the rest of his life with her. His wife, it seemed, knew about it but, as she said later, 'I did not consider it any of my business.' Open or not, his marriage to Alex was troubled. He told his GP about having to take out two loans to cover his debts. He also claimed he was suicidal. But, at least according to the Crown, it was not his own life he plotted to end. Perhaps he thought that removing his wife from the picture altogether would solve all his problems. So he planned to murder her.

First, he bought seven bottles of tonic water and laced them with atropine, which he used in his work. Then, he placed the bottles back on the shelf at the supermarket. But this was merely a smokescreen. He intended to slip more of the deadly substance into his wife's drink the first chance he got and she would just be one of many cases of poisoning. Whether he intended to kill anyone other than his wife is unclear but it is worth remembering just how much was in the bottle bought by Mrs Sharwood-Smith.

But, even while he was conspiring to murder, events were conspiring against him. His only real mistake was not taking into account the video cameras dotted around the supermarket. But fate also played a hand. First, there was Dr Sharwood-Smith. Who could have predicted that the husband of one of the victims would be a medical man who could tell a bad case of flu from the symptoms of atropine? Or that friends visiting the Sharwood-Smiths would also have knowledge of the substance?

Also, Agutter's wife did not feel the need for a gin and tonic until the following Sunday. She had taken some wine before then but the grape was not part of his plan at all. It had to be gin and it had to be tonic, otherwise the smokescreen would be wasted. She did finally request the prescribed drink but the locum responded to his call far faster than he had anticipated. Although his call did not indicate any great urgency, the doctor had come round immediately. This, also, did not fit in with his plan at all. Atropine takes four hours to work its deadly magic and then disperse, leaving no trace in the body. Agutter needed at least that before his wife could be admitted to hospital.

The sharp-witted ambulanceman also played his part. Because of the speed of response, Agutter did not get the chance to throw the remains of the glass down the sink. The ambulanceman, James Rudyj, took it away for analysis, noting that for the first time Agutter's calm composure began to waver. Mr Rudyj and the locum also recalled that the heating was on in the house, despite it being the height of summer. The high room temperature, it was believed, would have accelerated the effects of the poison. When analysed, the drink revealed a far higher concentration of atropine than any of the bottles, suggesting to the Crown that the poison came not from any of the tonic water but had been placed directly into the glass.

Despite the claims that she was the object of the poison plot, Mrs Agutter stood by her husband, visiting him in prison and even getting to know his lover. She refused to believe her husband had tried to kill her, saying, 'Clearly, in a case like this, you would have to be incredibly brain dead not to think of all the options. . . . I have considered it but I have rejected it.'

And Paul Agutter, despite being held on remand, insisted he was an innocent man. He wrote to the Sharwood-Smiths saying his marriage was under strain but he had the love of a woman he hoped would become his wife when he was cleared of the charges. Unfortunately for him, his lover broke off the affair during the trial.

In January 1995, Dr Paul Agutter faced that trial at the High Court of Edinburgh. He insisted he innocently bought a bottle of contaminated tonic water from the Safeway store. He denied attempting to murder his wife. He even said he found it offensive to use the word mistress when referring to his alleged lover. He claimed he did not dial 999 when his wife took ill because he did not want to overload the emergency services. 'I would only telephone for an ambulance if I knew I was facing a life-threatening situation,' he said. But, after an eight-day trial, he was found guilty by a majority verdict of attempting to murder his wife by putting a massive dose of atropine in her gin and tonic. He was also found guilty, again by majority verdict, of placing bottles contaminated with the poison on the shelves of the supermarket.

Lord Morison faced him from high on the bench and told him, 'This was an evil and cunningly devised crime which was not only designed to bring about the death of your wife but also caused great alarm, danger and injury to the public.' He then jailed him for twelve years. Agutter met his sentence with no observable emotion.

Within six months he was back in court – this time appealing his sentence. His counsel argued that there had perhaps been a break in the chain of evidence – and that trial judge Lord Morison had not advised the jury accordingly. The appeal centred on the drink Agutter had poured for his wife, the one allegedly containing the high concentration of atropine. Along with the gin, tonic and the ice cubes, which were all poured by ambulanceman James Rudyj into a glass jar to be taken away, was a slice of lemon. The sample was taken to a forensic laboratory where it was then poured into a fresh container. However, when the prosecution produced this at the later trial, the slice of lemon was nowhere to be seen. This, coupled with queries over the official labelling of the sample, naturally led the defence to suggest that it was not, in fact, the sample taken from the Agutter house. The appeal insisted that the evidence relating to the drink should have been discounted completely by the judge.

The Appeal Court, however, disagreed. Lord Morison had, in fact, drawn the jury's attention to the problems with the drink and warned them to be careful with the evidence. Therefore, they felt there were no grounds for the appeal and Dr Agutter was sent back to the jail to complete his sentence.

In late 2002, he was released after serving eight of his twelve years. During his time inside, he was known as a model prisoner, working in the prison library and assisting other convicts with literacy problems.

11

BODY OF EVIDENCE

Stuart Hutchinson

The legal term corpus delicti is defined in *The New Oxford Dictionary of English* as 'the facts and circumstances constituting a breach of a law' and its etymology is given as 'Latin, literally "body of offence"'. However, it is often misinterpreted, especially in crime writing, as referring to the necessity of having a body where murder is suspected. And there is a general perception that a person cannot be tried for murder unless a body has been found. But this is not the case – there just has to be enough evidence overall to prove that a murder has been committed.

In 1936, Irishman George Ball was convicted of killing his mother with an axe. He claimed she had committed suicide by slitting her own throat and he had merely dumped the body at sea. Her body was never recovered but the presence of a bloody axe in his shed and the opinion of forensic scientists led to his being found guilty but insane.

The body of actress Gay Gibson was also lost at sea, this time off the west coast of Africa while she was travelling on the ocean liner *Durban Castle*. In 1948, Deck Steward James Camb was convicted of murdering her on the basis of blood, saliva and urine stains on the bedclothes. Scratches on his wrist suggested she had defended herself while he was strangling her.

In England, John George Haigh believed the corpus delicti canard so much that he disposed of his eight victims in vats of sulphuric acid. Police arrested him for suspicion of the final murder but the woman's body had been reduced to little more than sludge. However, her dentist identified the one remaining piece of evidence, her dentures. Haigh was convicted and hanged in 1949.

In 1970, Arthur and Nizamodeen Hosein were convicted of abducting and murdering Mrs Muriel McKay, wife of Alick McKay, depute chairman of the *News of the World*. Fingerprint evidence helped convict them of both charges, although no body was ever found due to the belief that poor Mrs McKay had been fed to some pigs.

Similarly, in 1954, Polish ex-soldier Michael Onufrejczyk was convicted of the murder of his business partner. He may also have been fed to the pigs on their Welsh farm. At his trial, the defence said he could find no case in English criminal history in 300 years where there had been a conviction without identification of at least part of a body. But the alleged victim, Stanislaw Sykut was nowhere to be found and there were mysterious bloodstains on the kitchen floor.

Perhaps ex-oilman Stuart Hutchinson believed he could not be convicted without a body, which is why he took the bloody steps he did to dispose of his wife. But he did not reckon on the determination of a Scottish father-in-law who stubbornly refused to accept his daughter had simply vanished – or the gut feelings of two Aberdeen cops.

On the surface at least, Stuart and Alice Hutchinson were a happily married couple. Alice Davidson had been married before, to an Aberdeen stone merchant, and had two sons. She had married too young and the union dissolved. Then, in 1979 when her boys were aged three and eight, she met Stuart Hutchinson, a widower with a young daughter. Hutchinson was a petrochemical engineer whose job was to help drain the North Sea of its lucrative oil reserves. He was handsome, he was charming and – with a salary of £60,000 per annum – he was well set-up. They shared a mutual interest in opera, becoming involved in some amateur groups in the Granite City. They fell in love and, in 1981, were married.

Three years later – she was thirty-four and he was thirty-nine – they became part of the British ex-pat scene in Spain, eventually buying a £180,000 villa in Fuengirola on the Costa del Sol. There they continued their singing activities, taking part in shows in the town's English Theatre. Alice also gave singing lessons at their home, the Villa Bel Canto – the House of the Beautiful Song. Meanwhile, her husband earned a few pesetas more acting as an agent for removal firm, Pickfords.

They were regulars at the cocktail and dinner parties that were an important part of the social scene for the Brits enjoying their days in the sun. They were a popular couple – a pleasure to be around. They seemed so perfect for each other. But, as so often happens, there was a darkness at the heart of their sunshine life. They argued but what couple doesn't? But there were also allegations of abuse and Alice's two sons later spoke of their stepfather's violent tendencies, claiming he beat them and, on one occasion, tried to drown the youngest in the swimming pool. Even one of Hutchinson's close friends said that, although he was one of the most generous men he had ever met, he also had one of the most violent tempers he had ever known.

According to the later case against him, that temper broke one night in February 1989 and led to one of the most macabre and unusual murder cases Spain has ever seen.

Stuart Hutchinson told his father-in-law, Jim Davidson, that Alice had left him. They had argued, as they often did, but this time Alice had walked out, taking two suitcases and £800 in cash with her. Even then, he said later, he was not surprised, as she had pulled such stunts before. She phoned, he claimed, about six days later and then again four days after that. Then he heard nothing more from her. He told Mr Davidson back in Aberdeen that Alice had gone to Seville to take up singing as a career in the opera house there. Later, he said that she was in London, trying to make a go of it in Covent Garden. But Mr Davidson did not believe his son-in-law. Neither he nor his wife, Jean, could accept that their beautiful daughter had just up and left without getting in touch. The very thought of the person they knew and loved doing this was inconceivable. So, when he had not heard anything from her after one week of learning of her disappearance, he set in motion the investigative process that would soon involve two police forces in two countries. He contacted Grampian police first and they, in turn, alerted Interpol who asked the Spanish authorities to look into the case of missing Alice Hutchinson. By now, the woman had been gone for over a fortnight but her husband had still not contacted the local law. He had, however, offered the daughter of a neighbour the pick of his wife's clothes. Clearly, he knew now that this separation was permanent.

Jim Davidson learned of this clothing clearout when he flew to Spain in late March. He also discovered that son-in-law Stuart had put the villa up for sale – and that not only had his daughter left behind some expensive jewellery, she had also failed to take her passport with her. How, then, had she managed to get to Covent Garden? To cap it all, she had left her beloved Scottie dog behind.

Meanwhile, Aberdeen cop Chief Inspector Alex Den was becoming intrigued by the case of the missing opera singer. He knew, through previous experience, that there was a statute that could allow him to investigate. Under Section 6 (1) of the Criminal Procedure (Scotland) Act 1975, any British citizen who may have committed murder abroad could be punished in Scotland. This, he felt, gave him the power to investigate and investigate he did, finding out that big-spending Alice had not cashed any cheques or used any credit cards since she disappeared. Neither did she send her mother any card or flowers on Mother's Day, which was unusual. Then there was the passport, the jewellery, the sale of the house – and the fact that Hutchinson apparently planned moving to Malaysia.

A not very pretty picture was forming and Stuart Hutchinson was very much in the frame. But there was still not enough for the Crown Office to authorise action through the Scottish courts. More evidence was needed and, to get that, Chief Inspector Den and

Sergeant Gordon Thomson would have to go to Spain. But the wheels of bureaucracy grind even slower than those of justice and, if they waited for the diplomatic paperwork to be completed, the trail on the sunshine coast would have frozen solid. Again Interpol proved its worth and arranged for the two Scottish coppers to be invited over to Spain in order to 'exchange information'.

The pair arrived in mid April and met up with their Spanish counterparts, Inspectors Jesus Pena and Alfredo Tarijuan. They got right down to business and Stuart Hutchinson was summoned to the local police office for an interview. Surprised to be greeted by two Scottish detectives as well as the local law, he insisted his wife had walked out after a row. But the detectives did not believe him although they knew they could not arrest him on instinct alone. They needed something concrete. They needed evidence. They needed a body. What they got was blood.

Hutchinson's maid, Gertudis Poras, had defied an order not to go into certain rooms of the Villa Bel Canto and had found bloodstains on the wall of the master bedroom. This information gave the Spanish authorities the reason they needed to search the house and, in the early hours of the morning, they descended on the villa, finding Stuart Hutchinson in bed with his new Dutch girlfriend. They also found the blood – on the mattress, on the walls, in the bathroom. It was obvious someone had tried to clean it up, even going to the length of painting over it but, as Buck Ruxton had discovered over fifty years before, blood is notoriously difficult to hide.

Almost two months after Alice disappeared, Stuart Hutchinson was arrested for her murder. It would be another three years before the case and all its gruesome details came to court.

It was true that they had argued, Stuart Hutchinson told police officers. But Alice hadn't walked out on him. There were no suitcases packed, there was no cash taken, there were no phone calls from her days later. He had lost his temper after she taunted him about his sexual abilities, he claimed, and he pushed her down. She hit her neck on a wardrobe and as she screamed at him with blood gushing from an open wound he suddenly lost it completely. Snatching a baseball bat he kept in the bedroom as a defence against intruders, he proceeded to beat her to death right there in the bedroom they shared, while his teenage daughter slept a few feet away in another room.

But then the real bloodletting began. He dragged the body into the en-suite bathroom where he pulled out the sink, leaving a gaping hole to the main drain. Then he unscrewed the door from its hinges and, using it as a makeshift mortuary slab, began the forty-hour dissection of his dead wife's body, the blood draining through the hole in the floor. It was hard going using a kitchen knife and a household saw but obviously not impossible. He burned the head in the fireplace and cut the body up into thirty-eight pieces. Some of the portions he put into empty paint tins. He then soaked them with petrol and set them alight in the garden after his daughter had gone to school. The incinerated remains were then dispersed in rubbish bins along the coast while the bones were strewn on to rubbish tips.

He had disposed of the corpse. If there was no corpse, there could be no evidence of murder. If there was no evidence of murder, there could be no trial.

But the bloodstains told a tale. The splash marks in the bedroom were indicative of someone being beaten with a blunt instrument – and, when confronted by police, Hutchinson blurted out the full story. He even used a dead dog and two legs of pork to show how he had disposed of some of the body parts. And then there were the neighbours who told of how he had turned up with burned arms and singed hair a few days later. He had been burning something in his garden, he told them.

But, three years later, Hutchinson claimed police had forced his confession out of him. According to him, they said either he went down for the murder or they would pin it on his daughter. He had been given no food or water during the interview and had not been allowed to sleep. There was no interpreter present and he was not allowed to see his lawyer for some time, he claimed. He further claimed he did not see the full statement before he signed it. He insisted his wife was alive and well somewhere and just not getting in touch with anybody.

His confession, however, was the central plank of the case against him. For a time, great stock was placed on the testimony of his by-then sixteen-year-old daughter who had been living with relatives in England since his arrest. There was some doubt as to whether she would appear in the Palace of Justice at Malaga, where the trial would be held, and the hearing was, in fact, postponed twice while lawyers tried to convince the young girl to appear. As a ward of the English courts, special permission had to be obtained from a judge and then airfares for both her and one of her grandparents had to be paid. The organisation Prisoners Abroad finally managed to arrange the flights and a representative accompanied the girl and her grandmother to Spain where the British media was waiting. The case, naturally, had excited tremendous interest in the UK and just about every major newspaper had sent journalists and photographers to cover the proceedings. The arrival of the young girl caused a sensation but she was whisked away in a car without speaking to anyone – although there were some unpleasant scenes.

According to one press report, there was an emotional father-and-daughter reunion in Malaga's jail where Hutchinson was awaiting trial. They hugged and kissed during the hour-long visit and Hutchinson was reported as saying it was 'the happiest hour since I was arrested'. With his daughter now in Spain and willing to give evidence, he said he could now face the trial with total confidence.

His daughter later gave interviews to Grampian Television and the Press Association and finally gave her evidence in secret. Ultimately, despite her father's confidence, that evidence was deemed unimportant. The only significant thing she told the hearing was that, for five days after her stepmother had disappeared, she was banned from her father's bedroom.

Hutchinson's defence was simple – without a body there could be no case. 'If they convict, it will be by suspicion only. There is no proof. If Mr Hutchinson chopped up the body of his wife at their home, it would be impossible that no trace was left of her,' insisted leading Spanish lawyer Pedro Apalategui in the months before the trial got underway.

Although it took almost three years for the case to reach the court, once they began, the proceedings were swift. It took only two days for the case to be presented to three judges. The prosecution outlined Hutchinson's confession and pointed out that there was a £200,000 life insurance policy on Alice Hutchinson. There was drama as one of her sons called his stepfather a monster and stormed out of the courtroom, leaving a stony-faced Hutchinson staring straight ahead from behind his cordon of three armed police officers. There was emotion as a still-grieving Jim Davidson looked his son-in-law in the eye from the witness box and said, 'You killed her, didn't you? I want him put away forever.'

But his lawyer fought gamely to the end. 'There is no body,' he insisted, 'so there can be no case against him . . . His constitutional rights were infringed by the manner in which the police took the confession.' He also said, 'You have to have material evidence to show that a crime has been committed. Don't let's condemn a person for a mere confession.'

But the prosecutor Mr Valentin Bueno said, 'There was too much detail for the confession to be false. Murder has been proved.'

In the end, Hutchinson was sentenced to twenty-four years in a Spanish jail. The judges said his claim that the confession was forced was 'absurd in an adult in full possession of his senses'.

Depending on which report you believe, he would either spend the time virtually in the lap of luxury because he had the money to pay for it or he would spend most of it at hard labour. He would, however, continue his studies of the law, which he began while awaiting trial. He was also ordered to pay £220,000 compensation to Alice's parents and sons. He was led away still proclaiming his innocence.

But, for Jim Davidson and his wife Jean, it wasn't about the money – it was about justice. As far as they were concerned, he got what he deserved – although Mr Davidson was reported as saying that it was a pity garrotting was banned in Spain. But whatever his sentence was, it would never bring their daughter back.

Finally, despite their hope that he would be put away for a very long time, Stuart Hutchinson amazingly served only four years and nine months. His twenty-four-year sentence for wife-murder was reduced to fourteen years for homicide and then, following further changes in the Spanish penal code, he was eligible for early release. In October 1996, he was a free man once again although his lawyer was quick to point out that it was a conditional release and that, if he reoffended in any way on Spanish soil, he would be hauled back inside to complete his term.

And, finally, according to press reports, he admitted murdering Alice. 'I killed her,' a Spanish newspaper reported him as saying. 'Let's lay that ghost to rest. Now I am free to make a new life and do what I really want to do. The seven years I was married to Alice were another kind of hell.' She had goaded him with a string of lovers, he claimed, and he had killed her. Now all he wanted to do was continue studying to become a lawyer and remain in Spain.

But, for Alice's family, his early release was no kind of justice. They were stunned and horrified that the man, who had brutally murdered and disposed of their loved one in such a fashion, was free to get on with his life.

For them, the ghost would never be laid to rest.

12

MARRIAGE CONTRACTS

1.Veronica Little, Elaine Haggerty and William McKenzie

There are those who say that David Little brought his violent end on himself and perhaps there is something in that. According to the evidence produced at the trial, he was abusive to his wife to such an extent that she suffered a miscarriage. It was also revealed that he had seduced and beaten a teenage convent girl. His sexual appetites, which had led to an earlier conviction for rape, were his downfall for they forced his beaten wife and frightened teen lover into an unholy alliance.

One November night in 1981, the dark passions he had sparked ignited in a blaze of gunfire and David Little died in the garden of his young lover's home. The subsequent trial was filled with allegations of seduction, rape, lesbian love and murder for profit.

David Little met the woman who would become his second wife while he was on day release from Dumfries's Crichton Royal Hospital. In 1977, the local girl became Mrs Veronica Little, unaware that her charming new husband had, four years earlier, been convicted of rape and sent to the State Hospital at Carstairs for an unlimited period of time. When she met him, he had been deemed well enough to return to society and was attending the Dumfries hospital to prepare for his release. In October 1977, they had a daughter but it was not long after that that Little's Mister Hyde rose to the surface again. According to his wife's evidence in court, he seemed to resent the child. He often picked the baby up and shook her and threatened to put her 'in a pine box'. He began to beat his wife – on one occasion, he broke her nose and, on another, he kicked her so badly that she had to have a spinal operation. Forever after, she walked with a limp.

Then she became pregnant again but carried the child for six months before she lost it. The night she returned from the hospital, she later claimed, her husband raped her. Finally, she attempted suicide by taking an overdose of sleeping pills.

In November 1980, David Little embarked on an affair. Fifteen-year-old Elaine Haggerty had been motherless since she was nine and looked on Veronica as a surrogate mum. A pupil of the Benedictine Convent School, she began to baby-sit for the Littles to make some extra pocket money but she also ended up in a sexual imbroglio and, in her diary, she carefully noted the times and places she and David Little had sex. She wrote the journal in code but police officers later found a key to the code and were able to decipher it. They discovered that Little had seduced the young girl and had sex with her in cars, in woods and in his own bed after she had been to church. Then she found out she was pregnant. In a letter, Little told her she should consider having an abortion but she also lost the child.

Little, it seemed, beat his lover as well as his wife and, at some point, the two battered and abused women got together. Perhaps, at first, it was to show mutual support and compassion but, according to newspaper reports, their alliance also took a more physical nature.

Finally, though, thoughts turned to murder.

A letter was read out in court and, in it, Veronica Little told a friend she prayed for her husband's death. She also wrote that she was getting a divorce. 'What kind of man is that?' the letter read. 'I pray to God to take it from this earth.' However, it wasn't God who finally took David Little, it was five deadly .22 bullets tipped with gold.

The two women were to be joined by eighteen-year-old William McKenzie, a local youth with a crush on Veronica Little. The third member of this unholy trinity was a part-time soldier with ambitions to join the army full-time or become a gamekeeper. He was described as something of a dreamer. The prosecution suggested that Veronica Little used his sexual attraction to her to lure him into a plot to murder her husband. They also said that he was paid £120 for committing the murder – the cash was to be used to take him on a trip to America and Japan where he would study martial arts.

McKenzie, according to the police, confessed to his involvement almost as soon as they arrested him at the Territorial Army training camp at Glencorse Barracks near Penicuik. He said it had been Haggerty who had approached him with the idea. She told him that, as well as beating up his wife, David Little had also beaten her up in the past and had threatened to kill her. She said Veronica would pay him £120 if he would kill the man.

At 11pm on 25 November 1981, McKenzie was outside Elaine Haggerty's house, he told police. He had his .22 rifle with him and, when he saw David Little in the garden, he shot him. Little fell but then got up again and ran towards McKenzie. 'I shot him twice more and when he went down I walked up to him and shot him again in the head,' he allegedly stated.

The dead man was piled into his own car. The car was then driven out of Dumfries to a secluded lay-by where the body was dragged out and buried in a shallow grave. The bullet-riddled corpse was found later by a girl out riding. McKenzie's statement went on to claim he was given £70 by Mrs Little and Elaine for doing the deed while a further £50 was lifted from the victim's own wallet. He claimed Elaine promised she and Mrs Little would take the blame if the murder were discovered, as it was they who wanted the man dead. But, later, he changed his story. He admitted the murder weapon was his but he said he had lent it to Elaine Haggerty, along with eighty-five rounds of ammunition, so that she could use it to shoot rabbits. He claimed that he had confessed to the killing only to protect Veronica. It was Veronica, he said, who had actually pulled the trigger. All he had agreed to do was help to move the body into the car and dispose of it. He thought the man would already be dead by the time he got there but then he saw him in the garden, alive and well – but not for long. Veronica, he now claimed, grabbed the gun and shot her husband. He went down with the first shot but got back up again and staggered back towards the house, clutching his back. Mrs Little kept on shooting until her husband pitched forward and did not move again.

Veronica insisted that McKenzie shot her husband after he learned he had beaten her up. McKenzie, it was claimed, had become incensed by David Little's maltreatment of his wife and had decided to kill him. But the prosecution found out that Veronica had withdrawn cash from her building society account on the day of the murder – and, to compound matters, McKenzie had lodged the same amount in his account.

Elaine Haggerty, meanwhile, alleged it was McKenzie's idea to shoot the man.

At the trial, the various defence teams did their best to blacken the name of the victim, who obviously was not present to defend himself. In the end, the jury of nine men and six women took ninety-eight minutes to reach their verdict – all three were guilty of the murder of David Little. Veronica and William McKenzie were sentenced to life and Elaine was to be detained without limit of time – although, in theory, this meant she could actually be released before either of the others. As the judge declared sentence, Mrs Little trembled visibly and along with her young female friend wept openly. McKenzie just smirked at the court. There were gasps of shock from the public gallery and at least one female juror was in tears. Mrs Little cried out, 'God help us!' and slumped in the dock. Both she and Elaine had to be helped out of the courtroom.

Despite his outward composure, McKenzie must have been stunned by the verdict. He had earlier predicted that the jury would not be out long and, when they returned, it would be to deliver not guilty verdicts all round. However, he had also allegedly told prison officers that he had 'reached the top as a hit man'.

Like all such cases of murder, the so-called Dumfries Love Triangle case was a sad affair in which sexual desire was mixed with violence. Perhaps David Little did bring his violent end on himself. Perhaps William McKenzie's hormones did get in the way of his good judgement. Perhaps Veronica Little and Elaine Haggerty felt there was no other way out of the abusive relationships in which they had found themselves.

In the end, four lives were ruined that blood-spattered November night. And a four-year-old child was left without her parents.

2. George Carlin and James Nicholas

When chargehand Stephen Kane clocked on for work at Bothwell Bank Sewage Works one January morning in 1993, he had no idea he was going to uncover a grisly crime. At 7.45 a.m., his first job was to check the screens that catch any large items that often find their way into the system. On this day, there was something very large indeed blocking the screens. At first, he thought someone had chucked a tailor's dummy into the works but, under the glare of a car's headlights, he and his workmates saw that what was trapped in the screen was no dummy. It was a body with a piece of blue plastic rope wrapped round the torso and a shoe still on one of the feet.

Police were alerted immediately, of course, and they began the distasteful task of fishing the corpse out of a sea of sewage sludge. Once the remains were on terra firma, they discovered that the body was of a stockily built male of about five feet eight inches in height. They also saw that parts of the arms had been hacked off – although, at this stage, they could not say whether this was the result of the body's movement when it was in the sewage works or if they had been deliberately lopped off. What they did know was that this was an act of murder – something with which the Bothwell Bank Sewage Works was painfully familiar. Eight years earlier, a worker had gone on a murderous rampage and blasted three colleagues with a shotgun.

This time, though, the trail would lead outside the plant to an eternal triangle and a contract with death.

The killer or killers had gone to some trouble to conceal the identity of their victim. In addition to the thirty-five injuries that the pathologist counted – including skull fractures – they had, at some point, attempted to burn the body. Dr Marie Cassidy, consultant forensic pathologist at the University of Glasgow, likened some parts of the corpse to 'a roast in the oven'. She said the heat to which it was subjected was so intense it had caused the bones to crack. The corpse was also heat stiffened – that is, the extreme temperature had caused the muscles to meld and contract on the flexor surfaces of the limbs. This had caused the hands to be raised up to the face and the legs to be bent into a crouching position – rather like a boxer in the ring.

The remains were in a very poor condition and were, in fact, coming apart even as she examined them. At this point, she could not say which, if any, of the injuries had been inflicted pre- or post-mortem. She did, however, find a spent .22 bullet lodged in the head – although the brain and other parts of the skull were missing. A further search of the sewage works by police unearthed some of the missing skull fragments and she was able to piece together a rough scenario.

The bullet had entered the head just behind the right ear. The gun had been fired at close range of the victim and had been aimed at a downward angle of between twenty and forty-five degrees. The gunman was perhaps standing no more than four feet away. However, without access to the murder weapon, that could not be certain. Death was either instantaneous or this shot was a coup de grâce.

The first task facing investigators was to establish the dead man's identity. Missing Persons files were scrutinised and finally they settled on George Hall whose disappearance the previous October had been reported by his brothers. He had scars similar to the ones found on the body's face and neck. He also had distinctive tattoos on his forearms and this could explain why the lower parts of the corpse's arms had been hacked off.

Mr Hall had last been seen on 9 October 1992 by his wife, Janine (not her real name). They had been out in Glasgow for a meal to celebrate her birthday when he became involved in an argument with a taxi driver. She had tried to intercede and her husband had cursed at her then stormed off. She had not seen him since and bluntly told police, 'I don't care if I never see him again.' When she made this statement, about one month after her husband's disappearance, she was living with another man, George Carlin. This George was a financial advisor and she had first met him when she and her husband were trying to fix up a mortgage. He said the last time he had seen Mr Hall was six weeks before the night he vanished.

If the police had any suspicions, there was little action they could take at that stage. They told the Hall brothers that, as they had no body and no evidence of foul play, they had nothing to go on. George Hall was an adult and, if he chose to go walkabout, there was little they could do about it.

But the discovery of the body in Bothwell changed everything.

They reinterviewed Mrs Hall and left her crying and distraught. Shortly after that, they arrested her and George Carlin. They also arrested two other men – James Nicholas and Raymond Allison (not his real name). Along with the others, they were charged with murdering George Hall. Allison and Nicholas were additionally charged with dismembering and burning the body and concealing it in the sewage works in a bid to destroy evidence and defeat the ends of justice. Allison was also charged with setting fire to the car allegedly used in the crime and disposing of the gun in the River Clyde at the Red Bridge near Blantyre Farm Road, Uddingston, and with attempting to induce witnesses to provide him with a false alibi.

All four denied the charges. Ultimately, only two would go down – George Carlin, who changed his plea to guilty midway through the trial, and James Nicholas, who admitted helping him to dispose of the body. The change of heart allowed George Carlin to tell the High Court in Edinburgh what had happened that night.

According to the defence, George Hall was a drug dealer and gun-runner who stashed his deadly wares in the Bluebell Wood near Drumchapel, a housing scheme on the north-west of Glasgow. He was known to the police and was actually wanted for questioning in regard to a chequebook fraud. Carlin claimed that he had once seen him in possession of an Uzi sub-machine gun and a Kalashnikov rifle. It was also alleged he owed a substantial amount of money to the Drummy Crew, a gang of drug dealers allegedly operating in the housing scheme. The suggestion was that it was this shadowy gang of crooks who had murdered him.

George Carlin had begun his affair with Mrs Hall in September 1991. Ex-Marine George Hall, he claimed, was not the sort of man you upset so, even when Janine left him in November of that year to live with Carlin in Eastwood, on the south side of Glasgow, they continued to keep their love a secret. Carlin was still giving Mr Hall financial advice and, if he ever suspected that there was something between them, things would turn unpleasant.

Mrs Hall's life with her husband was no picnic, it was claimed. He was abusive towards her and made her life a misery. However, the dead man's family said that they had never seen any evidence of such abuse. In March 1992, she decided to go back to her husband while the man she really loved looked for somewhere safe for them to live. All the while Carlin felt it necessary, for safety's sake, to go on with the pretence of being George Hall's friend.

However, in May 1992, while Carlin and Janine were on holiday in Miami, George Hall did, in fact, discover the affair. Threats were made, it was claimed, and police took them seriously enough to arrange an escort to pick the couple up at Glasgow Airport on their return. George Hall responded by lodging complaints against the police officers involved, accusing them of interfering in his private life.

Carlin and Janine went on the run for a while, dodging from hotel to hotel and friend to friend, all the time fearful they would turn around and find her irate and decidedly dangerous husband behind them. Finally, exhausted and broke, Janine decided to go back again to her husband for the sake of her one-year-old child. A nomadic existence was no life for an infant. But George Hall had not forgotten his old friend George Carlin. Although he did not know where he was, he did have his mobile phone number and would call him at all hours, making dire threats. Once, he said Carlin would be nailed to a tree, covered in petrol and set alight. And, he assured Carlin, all this would be done in front of the Carlin children.

Carlin said in court, 'I don't think you know what fear is until you're in that position.'

Finally, it was decided the best form of defence was attack and soon thoughts turned to striking at George Hall first. Carlin said he discussed his problem with pal Raymond Allison, who allegedly, at first, offered to have Hall's legs broken. This, however, was not deemed a strong enough measure. Carlin felt the only way he could have any peace was if George Hall was taken out of the picture completely. To be absolutely safe, Carlin said, they would have 'to take him off the planet'. So, with alien abduction not a likely option, murder was planned. The first idea was to lure Hall to a lonely spot somewhere and shoot him but that was rejected because Carlin felt the man would turn up with his gangster mates and it could turn into a bloodbath. Finally, they hit on the idea of drawing him to a Blantyre bar that Carlin had been planning to buy. 'If I could get him out to the bar, I was told he would not leave,' Carlin told the court.

So the plan was nudged into motion. Carlin phoned his

tormentor and suggested the meet. Of course, he had no intentions of facing the man, even in a crowded bar room. He sat in a car across the road and waited for Hall to climb out of a taxi, then dialled a number on his mobile and said to the man who answered, 'That's him, there.' He had no idea to whom he had been talking. Whoever it was, though, he knew his business as the lethal events in the pub could testify.

The bar in question was no threat to the city's top-class watering holes. Its customers did not come for the decor or the fancy cocktails or lemon slices in their bevvy. It was a place where people came to drink and to talk and to have a good time – and, perhaps, to escape, if only briefly, from lives that were going down the drain as fast as the dregs from the beer glasses they drank from. They watched the telly or they listened to the music thumping out of the jukebox while a fruit machine provided a back beat of bleeps and whirrs and the occasional tuneful clank of money dancing into the slot.

According to witnesses, George Hall sat, beside a woman, on a raised area towards the back. He did not pay any attention to the three men in smart coats as they pushed their way through the door. He did not notice the two who peeled off and positioned themselves near the fruit machine. He was probably unaware as the third man stood nearby and aimed something at his head from under his coat.

They say you never hear the one that gets you and we don't know if George Hall found out if this was true. Witnesses, though, reported hearing two faint 'popping' sounds so perhaps the killer had a silencer screwed onto the end of his pistol. George Hall fell forward, blood streaming down his face. One female witness thought he had hit his head on the table as he went down.

People thought the man was drunk and had simply slumped into unconsciousness. They thought the two guys who rushed forward and hauled him up were his pals taking him home. They didn't know he had been shot in the head and that he was dead or dying. The woman at his side shifted uncomfortably in her seat as he slumped to the table but she did not move. Whoever she was remains a mystery and it is likely she just happened to be sitting there at the time and had nothing to do with Hall.

As the man was dragged out of the busy bar via the small kitchen, someone appeared with a bucket and mop and cleaned up the pool of blood on the floor. Months later, forensic scientists found traces of that blood encrusted on the mop and bucket and, using DNA fingerprinting techniques, they were able to link it with the body from the sewage works.

James Nicholas was in the bar's kitchen at the time of the incident and he admitted assisting in the disposal of the corpse. He did not take part in the dismemberment or the burning but he did agree to help, which is how Hall's blood was later found on his clothing. He did not name any of the men responsible.

Ten minutes after he had alerted the hit man, George Carlin received a call on his mobile. 'That's it done,' said the voice.

George Hall was dead and his body was about to vanish.

According to George Carlin, everyone in the pub knew what was going to happen but that was unlikely. Conspiracies only work if as few people as possible are involved. The greater the number of people who know about a criminal act, the greater the chance of someone talking to the police. However, as it turned out, there were people doing some talking, people who were willing to implicate both Raymond Allison and James Nicholson. One said that Nicholas had asked him to help clean up the blood. He also claimed that he told Allison, the morning after the shooting, that it had been 'out of order', to which Allison allegedly replied, 'No, it's all right – everything's all right.'

The same man also claimed that Carlin had paid him £5,000 for sorting two men out. However, the witness said he used the cash to go on holiday and buy a car and had no intention of sorting anyone out. But, in court, the witness claimed that police had threatened to charge him with the murder unless he implicated Raymond Allison in his taped interview.

179

George Carlin, who had admitted being part of the murder plot, was sentenced to twenty-five years. James Nicholas, who admitted assisting with the disposal of the corpse, was given five years. Janine Hall, exonerated by Carlin's testimony, had her not guilty plea accepted by the Crown. Raymond Allison walked from the court a free man. In his testimony, George Carlin had implicated him in the slaying but, under Scots Law, that was not enough to convict him.

'I do not know what you made of that,' the trial judge, Lord Caplan, told the jury, 'but that is not the point because, under our law, it would have to be corroborated. There would have to other evidence to enable you to decide, if it was your inclination to do so, that Carlin was telling the truth about Mr [Allison].' The judge went on, 'In my view, there is no corroboration. There is quite insufficient evidence to corroborate what Carlin said. Whether he was telling the truth or not, and I do not know, the accused cannot be convicted on that evidence.' Allison was subsequently convicted of a firearm offence in an Airdrie pub.

The murder trial was one of the most gruesome heard in many a long year in Scotland. It had been expected to last for several weeks but, in the end, thanks to the change of heart by Carlin and Nicholas, it lasted for just over three weeks – and that included a two-day delay because one of the jurors took ill. By that time, the jury had already been reduced to fourteen – also due to illness.

Whoever pulled the trigger in the Blantyre bar that night has never been caught. George Hall's family put up a reward for information but no one was ever arrested. There are suspicions – there always are – but suspicions are not evidence. The hit man, whoever he was, had got away with murder.

BIBLIOGRAPHY

BOOKS

Adams, Norman, *Scotland's Chronicles of Blood* (Robert Hale: London, 1996)

Bailey, Brian, *Hangmen of England* (W H Allen: London, 1989)

Browne, Douglas G and Tullet, Tom, *Bernard Spilsbury, His Life and Cases* (Harrap: London, 1951)

Dowdall, Laurence and Marshall, Alisdair, *Get Me Dowdall* (Paul Harris Publishing: Edinburgh, 1979)

Forbes, George and Meehan, Paddy, *Such Bad Company* (Paul Harris Publishing: Edinburgh, 1982)

Gaute, J H H and Odell, Robin, *Murderers' Who's Who* (Harrap: London, 1979)

Gaute, J H H and Odell, Robin, *Murder Whatdunit* (Harrap: London, 1982)

Glaister, John, *Final Diagnosis* (Hutchinson: London, 1964)

Grant, Douglas, *The Thin Blue Line* (John Long: London, 1973)

Hodge, James H (ed.), *Famous Trials* (vol. 4) (Penguin: London, 1954)

Hodge, James H (ed.), *Famous Trials* (vol. 10) (Penguin: London, 1964)

Huson, Richard (ed.), Sixty Famous Trials (Daily Express: London)

Hyde, H Montgomery, *Norman Birkett* (Hamish Hamilton: London, 1964)

Knox, Bill, *Court of Murder* (John Long: London, 1968)

Lane, Brian, *The Murder Guide* (BCA: London, 1991)

Lane, Brian, *The Encylopedia of Forensic Science* (Headline: London, 1992)

Livingstone, Sheila, *Confess and Be Hanged* (Birlinn, Edinburgh 2000)

Newton, Norman, *The Life and Times of Inverness* (John Donald: Edinburgh, 1996)

Pierrepoint, Albert, *Executioner: Pierrepoint* (Harrap: London, 1974)

Prebble, John, *The Lion in the North* (Secker & Warburg: London, 1971)

Roughead, William, *Twelve Scots Trials* (Mercat Press: Edinburgh, 1995)

Roughead, William, *Malice Domestic* (Greene and Son: Edinburgh, 1928)

Smith, Robin, *The Making of Scotland* (Canongate: Edinburgh 2001)

Smith, Sidney, *Mostly Murder* (Harrap: London, 1959)

Tod, T M, *The Scots Black Kalendar* (Munro & Scott: Perth, 1938)

Unknown author, *A Complete Report of the Trial of Dr E W Pritchard* (Wm Kay: Edinburgh, 1865)

Whittington-Egan, Molly, *Scottish Murder Stories* (Neil Wilson: Glasgow, 1998)

Wilson, Alan J, Brogan, Des and McGrail, Frank, *Ghostly Tales and Sinister Stories of Old Edinburgh* (Mainstream: Edinburgh, 1991)

Wilson, Colin and Seaman, Donald, *The Encyclopedia of Modern Murder* (Arthur Barker: London, 1983)

Young, Alex F, *Encylopedia of Scottish Executions 1750–1963* (Eric Dobby: Edinburgh, 1998)

BIBLIOGRAPHY

NEWSPAPERS

Caledonian Mercury
The Daily Record
Edinburgh Evening Courant
Edinburgh Evening News
Glasgow Courier
Glasgow Evening Times
The Glasgow Herald
Inverness Courier
Press and Journal
Scotland on Sunday
The Scotsman

ARCHIVE MATERIAL FROM THE NATIONAL ARCHIVE OF SCOTLAND

JC1/13, AD14/35/19, JC11/83, AD14/78/341, JC27/171, AD14/57/123, JC13/98

INDEX

187

INDEX

INDEX

INDEX

INDEX